Date Due			
May 11 '43			
May 15 '43			
May 10 '44			
May 10 '44			
Apr 23			
May 7			
May 22 '50			
May 11 '54			
Aug 23 '61			
Feb 28 '66			

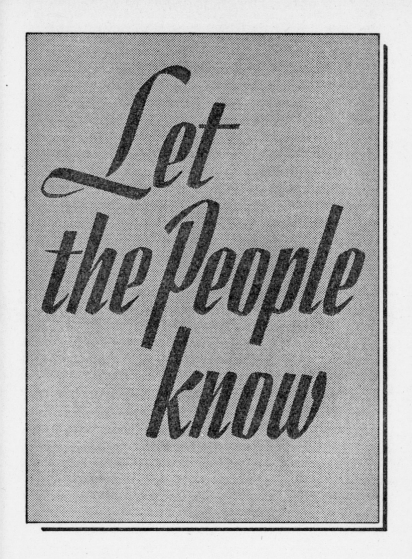

Let the People know

BY NORMAN ANGELL

NEW YORK · THE VIKING PRESS · MCMXLIII

April 1943

Author's Note

THE AIM of this book is to present and answer the questionings, doubts, and misgivings about the war, its causes, origins, and outcome which are present in the minds of immense numbers of average Main Street Americans, even when not expressed for fear of being regarded as defeatist or unpatriotic.

The questions have a decidedly isolationist slant—for the isolationist doubts have not been answered; only silenced by the bombs at Pearl Harbor. But to silence is not to answer. Many feel it has not yet been explained why we have any good reason to suppose that the next peace will be better than the last; why the slogans about this being a war for democracy should be believed when experience has shown that the self-same slogans in 1917—just as current then as now—turned out to be utterly untrustworthy.

An exceedingly strong case is presented for isolationist doubts and misgivings, in order that, in the rest of the book, the case can be plainly answered. The answer will show the isolationist case to be fallacious; it will show, moreover, that it is isolationism (European as much as American) which has produced this war; and that ordinary common sense and honesty, if placed above our prejudices, would have enabled the ordinary man to see the fallacy of our policy and to have avoided this war with its world-wide torments.

Indeed, the underlying proposition of the book is that the war has come upon us because we have rejected the elementary social truth upon which all humane society is based, namely, that the most primary right of all—the right to life, the right not to be killed and tortured—can only be made a reality by the general fulfillment of an obligation, the obligation of men to defend that right on behalf of others. The community as a whole, men collectively, must defend the right of each to life, or that right cannot be defended at all. Individual defense is in the long run a physical impossibility. If each individual—whether individual person or individual nation—takes the position that he will fight for his own life but not for others, then any violent minority can, by ganging up, subdue a vast majority, for it can apply "the simple and deadly plan of one by one": ten men can overcome a thousand if each of the thousand says: "I will fight for myself alone." For in that case the ten do not face a thousand, they only face one—one at a time.

Here is a truth quite undeniable, quite self-evident, vindicated again and again in human experience, particularly in political experience; a truth which more than anything else whatsoever explains the success of the Nazi Party in conquering, first the German nation and then, through that nation, the whole of continental Europe, reducing it all to impotence. Had we seen this truth after the last war, as some did see it, and acted upon it, not necessarily by forming a League or a Federation, but in the day to day conduct of the foreign policy of states (a policy which, in the last analysis, as in America's rejection of President Wilson's proposal, is shaped by the general drift of public opinion) there would have been no war. That principle might have been asserted on many occasions after the rejection of the League—by aiding China in 1932 (as we are now aiding her ten years later); by thoroughgoing opposition to Italy's Ethiopian aggression through sanctions in 1935 (in 1941 Britain opposed her by hard pressed armies in Africa); it might have been asserted in Spain, and again, the assertion, early instead of late, would almost certainly have prevented the present world war.

It was not asserted because this truth, so simple, so vital, is not merely not recognized, not admitted, but is commonly denied with deep passion, with all sorts of obscure hates and prejudices invoked in support of its rejection. It has been rejected alike by conservatives as being internationalist and antinationalist; by socialists as irrelevant to the task of destroying capitalism; by Peace Societies and pacifists as carrying the risk of war.

Why do the mass of men thus reject the simple, almost self-evident truths which might save them? Until we have answered that we cannot pretend to have given hope that even democracy can be a dependable system of human association.

Many reformers and democrats reject the belief that the ideas of the ordinary man constitute the supreme and fundamental factors of politics; while many intellectuals deny that it is within the capacity of ordinary busy men and women to have sound political judgment. Yet essential wisdom is possible without elaborate learning. (Lincoln did not need to have a college education in order to be wise.) The evils which have come upon us are not due to lack of knowledge in the sense that we lack the knowledge to cure cancer, or communicate with Mars, but are due to our failure to apply the knowledge we all possess to the guidance of public policy; we evade the self-evident—or it evades us—because we are not honest with ourselves in facing the facts of our own nature; we are encouraged alike by demagogues and by intellectuals to find scapegoats such as foreigners, or capitalists or bankers or big business or Jews, so that we may blame the evils of our society upon them, and not upon our own shortcomings. Democracy can never work so long as, refusing to face human shortcomings, we are content to say "The voice of the people is the voice of God." (Is the voice of the German people, the *Herr-envolk*, the voice of God?) Democracy will have a chance when we have the courage to say: "the voice of the people is very commonly the voice of Satan,"—the voice of resentment, prejudice, passion; for then we shall be on the watch for those demons and recognize the obligation to restrain them.

Seldom is John Citizen told that there can be no hope for democracy so long as we assume that none of us (for we are all "the people") need face the ugly facts of our own nature, our infinite capacity for evading plain truth because to do so might make it less easy or less pleasant to indulge some old atavistic animosity or grudge. Seldom is he told that the heaviest price of freedom is the giving up of some freedoms; that independence can now never be absolute; that all must be content with what each regards as less than complete justice to himself; that to claim the right to be sole judge of what is justice for ourselves is the sure means of doing injustice to another.

This book offers no panacea, no perfect blueprint, no short cut to the millennium. But by showing where and why public judgment went wrong after the last war, it may furnish aid for avoiding those errors in the future; help the plain citizen to do what he may to make our victory certain, and our peace less futile than the last.

Contents

John Citizen puts questions which are still in most people's minds but which many dislike to ask. He explains why he ought to have an answer the plain busy citizen can understand.

CHAPTER I

The Questions

THE writing of this book has been prompted mainly by the character of questions, constantly repeated, that have been put to the author ever since the war, by readers, radio audiences, classes of university students. He has been struck by the way in which the same queries kept on recurring; were repeated, in some cases, long after Pearl Harbor. Moreover, questions which few liked to voice publicly since Pearl Harbor were put with suggestive frequency and insistence privately. They often raised issues which at bottom were precisely those he had heard discussed more than forty years ago by American workers, when he himself was a hand on American farms and ranches.

These issues directly affect the war, not only in its ultimate purpose, but in its conduct and strategy. The public debate about them —and it was a debate upon which the country was deeply divided, and had been for years—may in large measure have been silenced by the bombs which fell on Pearl Harbor. But to silence a discussion is not to answer the questions which provoked it. They remain; the doubts and differences which gathered about them are still largely unresolved; they still affect morale and may suddenly come alive at a juncture where either the success of the war itself or the achievement of its purposes, may be put in jeopardy by confusions of public opinion—just as such public confusion on the occasion of the last war contributed so largely to the defeat of the main purpose for which it had been fought.

Some of those questions are gathered into a systematic list at the end of this chapter. But their human meaning, their bearing upon the lives of the anonymous millions, can better be understood perhaps by hearing one particular John Citizen put his case as he did

3

to me (though not all at once), presenting it, with perhaps just a trace of resentment, in about these terms.

The Case of John Citizen

You see, he explained, John II has finished his camp training and has now gone off, whether to Ireland, or Australia, or India we don't of course know. And he has left John III behind, John III being just two years old, as John II was three years old when I went off to France twenty-five years ago to fight World War No. 1.

What I want to know, of course, is whether that kid, now crawling in his rompers, will be haled off in twenty-five years' time to fight World War No. 3, just as his father has been haled off to fight World War No. 2, and his grandfather was haled off to fight World War No. 1; whether his business, his career, his marriage, his family life, will all be at the mercy of some gang of bad men on the other side of the world, or some gang of incompetents here, as his father's business, career, marriage, family life now is, and as his grandfather's was a quarter of a century ago.

Frankly I am more afraid of the incompetents over here than of the bad men over there—the incompetence of the big shots, the higher-ups, the wise guys. What have they been doing this twenty years, or not doing, so that though we had the Germans utterly licked at the time I came home, my son has now to go out and do the job all over again? We soldiers did our job; we then left the business to the politicos. With this result.

Nobody, so far as I know, even pretends to be able to answer the question whether it is all going to happen again or not. Nobody even tells us what we shall have to do in order to be reasonably certain that John III won't have to go off as his father and grandfather were obliged to. The wiseacres, from all I can gather, are in complete disagreement about what we ought to do about it.

But what I do resent is this: When I ask those questions, and say that we ought to have an answer, some fellows tell me that I'm not patriotic; that, since we are now at war, I ought not to worry what it's about, or attempt to understand its causes or its likely outcome; that all we now have to do is to obey, without question.

Well, it sounds singularly like the Hitler doctrine, in a war where the battle cry is democracy. If we are to get the habit of not asking questions what are we having the elections for? I've been a soldier—and may become one of sorts again before this show is over—and in the ranks I obey without question. But out of the ranks I am more than a soldier, I'm a citizen also. And as a citizen I'm supposed to give the orders—give the orders to the politicos, the government; to tell this big shot or that whether he is to remain a big shot or not. If I'm to give the orders—as in a democracy the voters, the little men must—then I want certain information. Or my orders are likely to go haywire.

The first bit of information I want is why we have to go through this business all again. We licked the pants off Germany more than twenty years ago. American troops occupied her territory; she was down and out. We could have made any kind of peace we wanted. The America of that day certainly did not want another war in twenty years' time. Why have we got it? Who or what is responsible? What were the mistakes that the government of that day made?

Certainly, the people did not want war. If this war comes out of their misjudgments about the League or the Court or Disarmament or what not, why did not those who are supposed to inform public opinion—the pastors and masters, the professors and writers and editors and columnists, the statesmen and politicians, the preachers and leaders—make it clear that we were running onto the rocks? Some of the highbrows who afterward wrote books to explain it all told us that the war came because American bankers wanted to save their bonds; or because Great Britain was determined to put an end to the trade competition of Germany and widen her own empire for further trade; and after the last war they also explained that one of the main reasons why the United States could not join the League was the badness of the Treaty of Versailles, that the League was being used by the victors for purely selfish purposes; that Wilson had been utterly bamboozled by the smart Europeans.

If this is true, what precautions have been taken this time to prevent a repetition of the tragedy? If the United States was powerless to prevent this collapse of the peace last time, what reason have we to suppose she will have power to do so next time? And if the collapse is due to errors made by the United States as well as by others, what kind of errors? Ought we not to know them in order that we shall not repeat them?

Actually at this moment our boys are fighting—in Australia, in India, and elsewhere in British territory—to defend and prolong that self-same British Empire against which our forefathers fought to be free. It is something of a paradox, to say the least. I've seen it stated twenty times that this war has come because Britain owned too much of the world and other nations too little; that it is a war between the Haves and the Have-nots; a war which came because Germany and Italy and Japan did not have access to raw materials. If so, why should not the Japs rather than France have Indo-China? The population there would probably just as soon be part of an Asiatic Empire as a French one. Are we fighting to keep Indo-China French? Just before our boys went to Burma, the Burmese were in rebellion against the British, just as the Americans were once. Are we quite sure the Burmese would rather be British than Japanese? Where did we get the information?

And the people of India: they have made it pretty plain that they did not care much about being protected either by Britain or ourselves; and some of their leaders have made it pretty plain that they don't want to fight the Japs very much. Indian property must not be destroyed. But my boy may have to give not alone his property but his life to defend India. When I read the other day that the negotiations between the British and the Indians had broken down, I knew that thousands of Americans would die as the result. But I also read that America must not interfere in the negotiations. But if we had no right to interfere, why are our boys in India? And then, when we have defeated Japan, just how are we to prevent her in a few years' time making the kind of comeback in Asia that Germany has made in Europe? Germany was utterly licked in 1918, and for several years afterward was broken, helpless, nearly starving. And then, a few years later, and under the noses of her former conquerors, she staged a comeback which enabled her in a few months to conquer the whole of continental Europe. She was able to do this mainly because her enemies—our allies—quarreled so much between themselves that they were simply unable to use their power for their defense; Germany simply picked them off one by one, destroyed them piecemeal. Will India and China, Burma, Malaya, Thailand, Indo-China have no internal divisions or divisions among themselves? Then their future is to be very different from their past, from all accounts. And if they are so divided, how will they be able to defend themselves from a renewed Japanese attack any more than Europe was able to defend itself from a renewed German attack? And even if they were united, could India, say, defend herself without the British Navy and China without American help?

The future choice does not seem an easy one for us. If, finding those countries by reason of their internal divisions, or their quarrels with each other, likely to lay themselves open to conquest, we take measures to defend them, we shall certainly be accused of imperialism; and if we don't do it, they may be conquered by Japan, as the recently defeated Germany has conquered Europe. In that case the vast resources of a country like India, with its four hundred million population, and its strategic position, will be used by Japan to threaten our own security.

This is a war for democracy. The word is shouted from every other column in the newspaper. But our chief ally, our main help at this moment, the ally to which a great part of our production is now going, is Russia. And although I don't agree with everything that Father Cassidy at the Catholic Church here used to say about Russia and its Communism before she became our ally, it is certain that Russia is no democracy in our sense of the term. She is a dictatorship, a dictatorship as complete as any in the world. The war began in Poland. It arose out of the guarantee given by France and

Britain to protect Poland if she were attacked by Germany. But for this guarantee, Poland, like Austria and Czechoslovakia before her, might have submitted to Hitler, and war might have been avoided. But Poland was hardly a democracy; she too has been most of the time, from all accounts, at least a semidictatorship, and the scene of some of the worst anti-Jewish pogroms of modern times. Was it worth setting the world on fire to "save Poland"?

All these facts bear on the question of what we are fighting for. And perhaps the future position of Russia, China, and India bears on that question still more.

Russia has put up a magnificent fight and we are all grateful to her. But it is neither fair to our boys and the safety of their children, and the fate of that new world for which we are fighting, to pretend that the possible future policy of Russia is not something we have to face very seriously. A complete defeat of Russia would be the signal for Hitler to make an offer for future "collaboration" which Russia might find very difficult to reject. Or, if not with Russia as a whole, then with these Ukrainians (there was a colony of them where I once worked out West) or other sections of Russia. We can hardly forget that for nearly two years of the war Russia was in a sense the ally of Hitler supplying him with materials; that she divided Poland with Hitler and that but for the prewar arrangement Stalin made with Hitler there might not have been a war at all. The Russian boys are pretty realistic, and in judging what turn their realism is likely to take we have to consider past experience.

But a great Russian success—for which I am ready to pray—would also present the makers of the next peace with a few headaches. If Stalin did succeed in completely smashing the German armies and in persuading the German population to rebel against Hitler, the rebellion thus created would of course be a Communist rebellion; the dominant party in Germany would be Communist, and it would look to Russia to help it impose its authority over the whole of Germany. You would then get Communism stretching right across the world from the shores of the North Sea to the Pacific. Much of

China has been Communist in the recent past; Nehru, the Indian leader, has declared that his sympathies are with Communism. Given this situation, the immense power which Russia revealed in the early stage of her war may mean at the peace the Bolshevizing of Germany and bordering states, China and India, constituting something like two thirds of the whole population of the earth. Is this what we are fighting for?

And as to China and India there is, I hear, to be no more discrimination against Asiatics; equality of economic opportunity for all. Does this mean that Chinese and Indians and other Asiatic or colored people are to be freely admitted to the United States? That our tariffs are to be so lowered as to admit freely goods produced on wage scales which are in some cases less than half of ours? Is this what is meant by equality of economic opportunity?

We are repeatedly told that if our people are to fight as they may have to, they must have a vision of a "New Order," a new world; that they won't fight merely for the kind of world and the kind of America we have known so far.

Well, I've known what it is to be out of a job, and some of my wife's people were farmers in the Dust Bowl, and some of *their* people were croppers down South. These things ought not to be; and I'm all for the New Deal when it tackles these problems. I believe F.D.R. has made a beginning. But when some of these college youngsters talk about the New Order from which all capitalism is to be abolished, I want to know what capitalism is and who are the capitalists that are to be eliminated. I am not sure that I know what they mean by these words. I run a garage; my brother a diner. We both managed to start with money saved from wages. Millions upon millions of Americans throughout the United States have done exactly that kind of thing. It is the kind of adventure they relish. Yet my young Communist friends tell me that I have exchanged wage slavery for capitalist exploitation and robbery because I now employ two men in the garage; and that for that offense I would be punished severely in Russia, possibly executed. Am I really to be treated that way in the New Order? My job in the auto works, where I saved the money to start my business, was not slavery for the simple reason that I could leave it. If the only employer is the state, and I were just a soldier in an industrial army, I could not leave my employment. If we are to use such words as slavery, I should be more of a slave in such an army than I am now. If I proved incompetent the boss in the auto works could fire me. In Russia, from all accounts, my incompetence might quite easily have been interpreted as sabotage and I might quite easily have been shot, especially if I had ventured to criticize the management. And I should almost certainly have been shot if I had indulged in criticism of the Communist party line of the moment. If the New Order that one hears about means that savings can never be used to start your own business and be your own boss, that your life through you must be at the orders of a committee or a commissar, themselves at the orders of other committees and commissars, who in their turn are at the orders of still more remote committees and commissars, then we shall not have moved nearer to freedom, even to economic freedom, but very much further from it. And I know—since I did not give up reading when I left school—that the freedoms which have made our American way of life possible have not been easily won; and I suspect that they may very easily indeed be lost.

But some of the wiseacres who were anxious to have us in this war have been contemptuous of those freedoms; they give us little assurance that in their New Order those freedoms can exist.

You say that it is unpatriotic to ask these questions? I say that there can be no sound and dependable patriotism until they are answered.

John's Questions Tabulated

Perhaps it will help to clarify things if we disentangle the questions in John's little speech, separate one from the other, and tabulate them—adding certain questions which cropped up in the course of conversation, but which have not been included in the above condensation of his talk. The list would then be about as follows:

*This is a war to make the world safe for democracy. So was
the last. But it did not do it. Why should this one?*

Are our boys fighting in India, Burma, Ceylon, Africa to
give those countries democracy, or to maintain the British Empire in those parts?

Why are we defending that Empire in Australia and New
Zealand and Africa and Ireland and many other places, when
our forefathers fought to be free from it, and did their best to
destroy it?

If we are fighting against dictatorship and totalitarianism,
what of Russia, which has always been a dictatorship whether
under a Czar or a Stalin? What of China where dictators or
war lords and not parliaments are the real rulers? Is not Russia's
dictatorship as bad as Germany's?

Many students have maintained these last years that the
power of financial interests supporting an astute British propaganda played a large part in involving us in the last war. Have
those forces been at work in involving America in this war also?

For years it has been commonly asserted that the European
victors in the last war used their victory, which American aid
made possible, for their imperialist purposes, adding greatly to
their territorial conquests. What assurance have we that that
experience will not be repeated?

Is it not true, as a distinguished American has said, that this
war has come because Britain owns too much of the world and
others too little? Because Italy and Germany and Japan have
neither enough raw materials nor sufficient outlet for their population? That it is a war between the Haves and the Have-nots?
Is it not a gross injustice that Britain—a nation of forty-five millions—should own a quarter of the earth?

If Russia, of nearly two hundred million people, and China,
of four hundred million, are victorious and join with India of

four hundred million, a good deal more than half the world's
land and population will form a bloc which has never in history known democratic institutions. Does the prospect look like
making the world very safe for democracy?

If Russia beats Germany, will not Russia dominate and direct
any future German revolution, giving it a Communist turn?
And if the New China and the New India turn toward Communism, as some Chinese and Indian leaders threaten, will not
Communism then dominate the world?

We know something at least of our own problems—the
trusts, labor, farming issues, social security—but how can the
American voter and the American Congress pass upon the rights
and wrongs of struggles in Europe, Asia, and Africa?

If we are drawn into these never-ending conflicts, will not
the very complexity of the issues make it necessary to withdraw
decisions from Congress? Does not power to decide foreign
policy inevitably mean power to decide all policies—domestic
and foreign alike—since foreign matters involve war, and once
at war, all domestic matters must yield to its needs? Is this the
way to make democracy secure?

If there are risks for American democracy in staying at home,
are there not greater risks still in being drawn into every foreign
complication?

If we do interfere in the politics of the whole earth, are we
to re-create the League we refused to have anything to do with
twenty years ago, or make a Union Now with other democracies,
or what?

If we unite with Britain do we not unite with the British
Empire also, and take responsibility for India, Palestine, Africa;
go, in fact, into the Empire business?

And if we federate with Britain and its Empire, what of the
king, and hereditary peers, titles, class divisions, and distinc-

tions—things which don't go at all well with the American tradition of republican and democratic equality we have maintained ever since we kicked the British king and the British aristocrats out of this country?

Or shall we have to share that brand of British Socialism which has grown up this last thirty years, with its dole, its vast unemployment insurance, its Labour party, its grueling income tax—all to be added, perhaps, to our own New Deal?

Does "equality of economic opportunity" mean that Asiatics are to be admitted freely to the United States and that goods made under the American standard of wages have to compete with goods made by coolie labor?

In attempting to group and systematize the answers to these questions the author found—as he expected to find—that clarification demanded that certain principles, recurring over and over again in the answer to many different questions, should first of all be uncovered, rendered visible. The effort to do that produced the chapters which follow.

The notion that John is the helpless puppet of the "interests" is a fallacy. His opinion is the final court of appeal in politics. The kind of leaders we get depends on him, since none can lead if he does not follow. It was he who defeated Wilson in America and helped in Britain to destroy the last peace—meaning well all the time. The "interests" have often been as blind to their interest as John to his; the "educated" just as wrong as the "uneducated," and John's common sense can often be a better guide than the expert's learning. To grasp the full meaning of the obvious is a better basis of sound judgment than confused knowledge of the obscure.

CHAPTER II

Can John Do Anything about It?

A GOOD many, on reading John's outburst, will be disposed to say that none of it makes any odds; that we are in the war; that the country had no choice about it after Pearl Harbor; that we have to see it through to victory; that both the main political parties are completely agreed on this; that no man can really say what will follow; that the Republican Party, as well as the President's party, has now abandoned all the old ideas of an isolationist America; that in view of this biparty agreement on the main issues, individual questioning like that in which John indulges does not really amount to a hill of beans, as he might put it; that the big shots will arrange it between themselves and that the common man will have nothing to say about it.

As to this alleged position of the common man in the waging of war and the making of peace, a few questions would seem to be in order.

If the opinion of the ordinary man makes no difference, why is it that even dictatorships like Germany, which have repudiated democracy, take such infinite pains to ensure that the common man shall think as the government desires him to think? Germany has devised the most elaborate apparatus of propaganda that the world has ever seen, in order to control the mind of the public. It begins in the nursery so as to ensure proper "conditioning" of the mind during childhood; continues in the school; every word and every thought that reaches the young German are such words and thoughts as the government deems desirable. Every book, every newspaper, every film, every radio address, every play, is shaped with a view to the formation of certain ideas. No German is allowed to read a paper or book or see a play or listen to a radio talk that has

17

not had the proper supervision; and ferocious punishment, including death, may be meted out for violation of the rules. No government in history has ever, perhaps, devoted so much money, attention, organization, science, to the problem of ensuring that the common man shall think as the Leader wants him to.

But if what the common man thinks has no importance why this vast expenditure, these elaborate and far-reaching measures?

The reply is of course that Hitler knows, better than we seem to know, that what the common man thinks is the first and last factor in politics; that if you can control what he thinks you can control what he does, and what his nation does. For "ideas are the foundation of action."

When Hitler started with his dozen fellow agitators he had no force; he had only the opportunity of going out and persuading (he could not force) a number of others to join him; they in turn persuaded others—various political parties, political leaders, industrialists. This "movement of ideas" was the beginning, the basis, of what followed.

Popular ideas, or ideas which could be made popular, were, of course, used particularly for creating divisions among the people, so that one party, or class, or race could be played off against another.

Manipulation of Ideas as a Military Weapon

Just as Hitler has recognized the enormous importance of John Citizen's ideas at home, he has used the ideas of John Citizen abroad as his supreme military weapon.

The basis of Hitler's relatively easy conquest of twenty nations is that he was able to take them one by one. If they had refused to be divided and had fought as a unit, he could not have overcome them. And the basis of their refusal to unite, the one overriding reason for the divisions which made Hitler's conquest so easy, was the popular sentiment of his victims, particularly that supreme popular sentiment of nationalism which one historian has described as "the most potent political force in Europe." Hitler knew that

everywhere in the world the John Citizens tend to be nationalist—
to find it difficult to get along with foreign nations, or to co-operate
with them. And he knew how to utilize that feeling of the common
man.

Note how this popular sentiment of nationalism—isolationism—
has influenced the events which played their part in precipitating
America into another world war.

There is coming now into rapidly growing favor the view that if
this country, instead of turning its back not merely upon the League
and the World Court, but upon any form of international co-operation after the last war, had stood for collaboration with other nations
in some peace-preserving organization, there would have been a
greater chance of preventing the totalitarian aggression. But the
enemies of the League, the Court or any other form of international
co-operation, were able to appeal to a strong popular sentiment, and
by means of it to defeat any form of internationalism. No one has
ever suggested that the "interests"—the bankers and the capitalists
—were behind the anti-League agitation. On the contrary it was one
of the main charges of the opponents of the League that Wall Street
and the interests were for it. The common charge was that it represented a foreign, a European, a British maneuver. [1]

We see here creeping into the situation an element in popular
opinion of which Hitler has made enormous use both in Germany
and abroad—the scapegoat element, the utilization of that tendency
to blame upon others difficulties or troubles more properly due to
our own mistakes. The anti-Semitism of the Nazi is no casual accident or incident. It is an important part of their psychological technique for dividing those who might oppose them, for turning blame
from themselves to a third party if things go wrong; and for preventing the growth of a rational public opinion, which, if thought

---

[1] Mr. Quincy Howe, among others, has no doubt at all that the League
was a device of "British imperialists . . . fashioned to protect their world-wide
holdings." His book *Britain Expects Every American to Do His Duty* is devoted
to explaining how, America having withdrawn from the League, the British
have been devising new schemes "to commit the United States to defend their
interests."

replaced feeling, might develop public capacity for a unified action which would make the Nazi domination impossible.

The thing which later in these pages I call "escapegoatism" is an indispensable part of that public bamboozlement which is part of the Nazi technique.

And there have been since the last world war scapegoats aplenty, turning attention from the real nature and cause of war, and the reasons for involvement in the present one. For a time the supreme scapegoat was the armament maker, the "merchant of death," those fifty evil men who for their base profits, compelled the supposedly helpless people of the world to go to war, in the face of all popular will to the contrary. During months Congress investigated their efforts to induce the country to arm itself more heavily. The final result of all the agitation is this: the very men who instituted it now insist that the merchants of death fell down shamefully and disastrously on their job. Senator Wheeler has declared upon several occasions since Pearl Harbor that his real indictment of the administration is that it took the country into war "unprepared." But "unprepared" commonly means that it had not armament enough. Everyone now wishes that so far as the United States and Britain are concerned, the armament makers, the merchants of death, had succeeded a great deal better than in fact they did.

The charge against the bankers during the prewar years was that they were interventionist, favoring co-operation with Britain; opposing the policy of isolationism for this country. But is not the present all-party, universal condemnation of isolationism, the universal recognition that Britain's capacity to resist Germany is an American interest, a justification of the very policy for which they were condemned? Is not the American government itself, in its efforts to persuade the public that the war against Hitler is truly America's war, doing later what those much blamed propagandists tried to do earlier?

What the isolationist senators and congressmen actually argued at the time of the passage of the Neutrality Act was that the armament makers "and other Wall Street interests" were opposing the popular isolationism of the time. One could now wish that they had been more successful.

The truth is of course that when an eminent author wrote a year or two since that "no reason for war remains except sudden profits for the fifty men who run the munitions racket," [2] he wrote what was immensely popular, all but universally accepted; and what was and is demonstrable nonsense.

If in fact these men had power it was by virtue of their influence upon public opinion. The fifty could not use force in the sense of physical compulsion. Fifty obese capitalists cannot force scores of millions: the force is on the side of the millions. The fifty wanted the millions to go to war. So be it. Why did the millions obey—take step after step extending over a course of years, in the way of congressional or parliamentary votes, added taxation, naval and military budgets, draft acts—all accompanied by long and public discussion, thousands of newspaper articles, radio debates, hundreds of books? In so far as fifty men engineered it at all, they could only act via the public mind, by persuading voters, and so Congress or Parliament, that the national interest demanded the creation of armament. The thing which gave them antisocial power—so far as they possessed it—was the confusion of the public regarding the appropriate policy of defense; and, what is more important, the confusions attaching to the accepted ideologies of national rights and sovereignty.

There is no evidence that such groups as bankers or big business had some special interest in plunging the world once more into war,

---

[2] The late Frank Simonds, reviewing a series of these books about the armament plotters, wrote most truly:

"It is what the people *en masse* accept as their rights, as the rights of their countries, sovereign and imprescriptible, and call upon their leaders to maintain uncompromisingly, that make wars.

"When, therefore, as in the present books, you start muckraking the arms trade, whatever useful reform you may accomplish in that direction, nevertheless you inevitably draw a red herring across the main trail. You help to sustain the individual in his comfortable belief that wars are made by wicked foreigners or dishonest natives, by the Hitlers abroad or the Zaharoffs at home. You start him full tilt after someone who is, in effect, only his own accomplice."

in policies that would lead to that result. There is a great deal of evidence to show that certain popular, widely spread, and deeply rooted convictions touching national rights and interests, sentiments like those of nationalism, dislike and suspicion of foreigners, have had most to do with creating the situation which led to war—and rendered a number of lesser democracies impotent to resist a large single nation like Germany. And there is a great deal of evidence to show that the bankers and big business and wearers of old school ties were just as much the victims of confusions about national right and obligation, and of nationalist mistrust, animosities, pugnacities, and other similar foolishness, as the simplest coal heaver, plumber, or garage hand.

If, indeed, the fifty did dominate the public mind, and so, public action, it was by bamboozlement, and our real problem in that case is to provide John Citizen some intellectual prophylaxis against bamboozlement. If his deception is as easy as authors of the school of thought just quoted would persuade us that it is, it will serve little purpose to get rid of the fifty armament makers, or a dozen or so bankers. With so easily gullible a public mind, their place would be immediately taken by some new exploiters.

When we talk of vested interests, we should remember that a politician's basic vested interest is a seat in Parliament or Congress; that a newspaper owner's chief vested interest is the prosperity of his paper, which depends, as the basis of its advertising revenue, upon circulation; and the circulation depends upon efficiently responding to the tastes and preferences of John Citizen. What John does about it determines alike the fate of the congressman and the newspaper. The ease with which, and the extent to which, those tastes and preferences—preferences in politics usually for having as little as possible to do with foreigners, for national isolation, independence—can be exploited by vested interests, depends, of course, upon the degree of John's gullibility as to what *his* interests in the matter are. To reduce that gullibility—which means commonly in practice reducing John's liability to be sent off on an emotional chase after scapegoats, visible devils like armament makers, bankers, international financiers, Jews—is, in the last analysis, the best, indeed, the only way to enable him to defend himself against the interests which might exploit him.

The Public's Part in War Making

Mr. Wendell Willkie has recently reviewed for us the facts in this matter, of the early postwar years. Woodrow Wilson, Mr. Willkie reminds us, produced a concrete program of international co-operation intended to "safeguard all nations against military aggression, to protect racial minorities and to give the oncoming generation some confidence that it could go about its affairs without a return of the disrupting and blighting scourge of war." Mr. Willkie adds:

> Whatever we may think about the details of that program, it was definite, affirmative action for world peace. We cannot state positively just how effective it might have proved, had the United States extended to it support, influence, and active participation.

> But we do know that we tried the opposite course and found it altogether futile. We entered into an era of strictest detachment from world affairs. Many of our public leaders, Democratic and Republican, went about the country proclaiming that we had been tricked into the last war, that our ideals had been betrayed, that never again should we allow ourselves to become entangled in world politics which would inevitably bring about another armed outbreak.

"As a result," says Mr. Willkie, "we sacrificed a magnificent opportunity for leadership in strengthening and rehabilitating the democratic nations, in fortifying them against assault by the forces of aggression which at that very moment were beginning to gather."

The responsibility for that result does not attach solely to any political party. The fight about the League, he goes on, "furnishes a perfect example of the type of leadership we must avoid in this country if we are ever going to fulfill our responsibilities as a nation that believes in a free world, a just world, a world at peace."

Mr. Willkie goes on to tell the story in some detail, thus:

When this question passed from the Senate to the two great political conventions of 1920, neither of them stood altogether for or altogether against the treaty as it had been brought home by the President. The Democratic Convention in its platform did not oppose reservations. The Republican platform adopted a compromise plank which was broad enough to accommodate those of any viewpoint respecting the particular Woodrow Wilson covenant. There were many firm supporters of the League in the Republican ranks. They found the platform altogether ample to give them standing room, while the anti-League delegates found safe footing there too.

The truth to which Mr. Willkie returns again and again is that *the people were confused.*

The platforms were ambiguous; the parties had no consistent historical position about the co-operation of the United States with other nations. The confusion was doubled by the attitude of the Republican candidate, Warren Harding. There was no doubt that Cox's position on the Democratic ticket was a fairly definite support of the Wilson treaty, though his party platform left open the possibility of reservations and many of the Democratic leaders were openly in opposition.

But no one was certain whether Harding was merely pulling his punches against the League or whether he intended to support it aggressively upon election in a modified form. In private conversation he gave each man the answer he wanted, and of his speeches the Republican National Committeeman from California, Chester H. Rowell, said:

"One-half of the speeches were for the League of Nations if you read them hastily, but if you read them with care every word of them could have been read critically as against the League of Nations. The other half were violent speeches against the League of Nations if you read them carelessly, but if you read them critically every one of them could be interpreted as in favor of the League of Nations."

It was not until after the election returns were in that Harding spoke frankly of the League as "now deceased."

As bearing upon the question how it came about that the desire and intention of a great people for peace were so completely frustrated, Mr. Willkie has this to say:

> I am satisfied that the American people never deliberately and intentionally turned their backs on a program for international co-operation in an organization for maintaining world peace. Possibly, they would have preferred changes in the precise Versailles covenant, but not complete aloofness from the efforts of other nations. *They were betrayed by leaders without convictions who were thinking in terms of group vote catching.*

Note this conclusion, the "people were betrayed by leaders without convictions who were thinking in terms of group vote catching." The point of the conclusion is this: the votes were caught, and if we, as voters, are not to be caught a second time, we must know something of the methods that were followed, what bait was used, why we swallowed it.

The bait was, of course, precisely the bait which after the war was offered to the people of Europe in one form or another and which they too, like the people of this country, swallowed: the bait of nationalism, isolationism, separatism, a pleasing absence of any obligation.

Side by side with Mr. Willkie's story of the course of the discussion of the League in America, might be put the contemporaneous story of the reparations claims of Britain and France—for the behavior of these two countries in that matter had an immense influence in setting the course of postwar events in a particular direction, a direction which produced conditions that favored the coming of Hitler.

The particular feature of the reparations episode which interests us here is this: on the whole, after the first burst of postwar anti-Germanism, the "interests"—the bankers, the "city," the capitalists—were in favor of doing the reasonable thing, while a largely tabloid-fed public were emotionally confused, and, dominated by a desire not to let the Germans off lightly; and so delayed for a full decade a settlement which, had it been made promptly, might have saved the Weimar Republic. In that case the world might have been saved from Hitler.

It will be recalled that after the last war the European Allies presented claims for astronomical reparations as against Germany; and that to the payment of the sums demanded certain conditions were attached: Germany was not so to increase her foreign trade as to compete with Allied trade either in home or in neutral markets. She was to pay, but pay in money, not goods. Everyone knew about how much gold she had: if the Allies had taken it all, it would have satisfied only about 1 per cent of their claim. I remember discussing the matter with certain men who afterward became my colleagues in the House of Commons and asked them to imagine that all Germany's gold had been seized, and that our tariffs were successfully preventing any increase of German foreign trade. How in that case was she to pay? The answer kept coming back "in money, not goods." One of my colleagues was sure that if he were given a free hand by the government he could soon collect the money. He would go, he said, with a few regiments and some motor trucks to Berlin, and notify the German government that unless the trucks were loaded by a given date with the money owing us, two members of the German cabinet would be shot; if, within a given period after the shooting, the money was not forthcoming two more would be shot. And so on. The author of this plan was certain that within a few weeks we would get "the money." I asked him to imagine that he had got it; that his plan had succeeded and that this money had been brought to London and Paris. What would he do with it there? We had agreed that all the gold had already been taken. This would be German paper money. It would be of no use in England. Neither butcher nor baker nor income tax collector would take German paper money. It had value in one place in the world only, Germany, where truly it could be exchanged for goods. But our statesman had imposed a condition about those goods: they were not to leave Germany, for Germany was not to increase her foreign trade. I suggested to him that what his proposal amounted to was that having collected this German money and brought it to London, he would have to distribute it to favored sections of the British population who thereupon would migrate to Germany with the money and stay there drinking German beer until the reparations were exhausted.

Is that point very difficult to see? It took the British public twelve years to see it (since the reparations matter was not really settled until the Lausanne Conference of 1932). The French never saw it. And certain American senators in respect of the British debts seem to have some difficulty in seeing it. Yet the fact of keeping open this economic sore for twelve years had an immense influence upon the course of economic events after the war. More than one historian has insisted that if the British and French publics had done in 1920 what they did in 1932, the German inflation might have been avoided; if the German inflation had been avoided Hitler would not have been able to exploit the miseries it brought; the world indeed might never have heard of him.

If there is any considerable element of truth in this—and there is —the future historian will have to note that one of the grave contributory causes of the collapse of Western civilization was the failure of the British and French publics, during twelve years, to understand a point in economics which could be made clear to any intelligent adolescent in twelve minutes.

This is surely an eloquent commentary on the way in which modern education prepares the voting millions who make and unmake governments, who send the world to war and make the treaties of peace—to understand the nature of the world in which they live, and by their votes, direct and manage.

Twenty years since this present writer delivered himself thus:

> The most powerful section of our Press has consistently done its best to keep from its readers the one fact which in the interests of European peace it was necessary to impress upon them. Many aspects of the economic problem in Europe are obscure and difficult. This crucial point is clear and simple. We want Germany to pay a certain large sum; she can only do so by greatly expanding her foreign trade.

Here is a simple truth, the more general realization of which might accelerate enormously the settlement of Europe and the solution of our own pressing economic problem. It is a national interest that it should be known. Not only have some of our largest papers not brought out its truth, they have persistently hidden it, and not only persistently hidden it, but they have insistently implied the exact contrary. Any day you may read stories of the way in which "money that ought to go to the Allies" is being spent upon public improvements, theaters, country excursions. "Why don't the Allies tax German amusements?"

It is a "little too thick" to assume that after years of discussion, of Bankers' Reports, expert explanation, the correspondents who send this kind of thing, the editors who print it, do not know that it has no bearing on the question of what Germany can pay; do not know that the printing of it merely helps to keep alive a confusion of mind that paralyzes the action of statesmen and prolongs a situation fatal to the nation's most elementary interests.

Side by side with that comment of the time, we may usefully put the comment of the American economists, Professors Bass and Moulton, of the University of Chicago, who wrote:

What hope is there for the world so long as the leading Premiers of Allied countries admit that Germany can pay only with goods which none of the Allied nations are willing to receive, and give support to their Parliaments in framing tariff measures designed to prevent German exports, at the same time insisting that recalcitrant Germany must meet the Reparation obligation to the last farthing and the last sou? What hope is there for the world so long as most of the leading students of international finance and economics, who recognize the fundamental illusion in Reparations and Allied debts, will frankly discuss the subject in undertones and in inner offices? What hope is there for the world when statesmen and financiers alike, while lacking the courage to tell the truth about Reparations and inter-Allied debts, insist that nothing can be done as a practical matter, "however desirable it might be from an economic point of view," because the people will not be satisfied to give up the supposed advantages of Reparations and debt payments? If ever there was a time for leadership in a campaign of enlightenment on the fundamentals of international economics it is now. If ever there was a time when the truth is needed to set men free, it is now. If ever there was a time when evasion and concealment were political virtues, it is not now.

Understanding of the debts question in America was then at about the same stage that the European understanding of the reparations question was in the decade following the Armistice. That is to say, the public saw hardly any connection whatever between the tariff and the payment of the debts; still failed to understand the fact which is at bottom self-evident—that if Europe were to pay its debts America must increase her imports.

It would distort altogether the case I am trying to explain—it would indeed turn it upside down—if I were to leave the impression that the policies which have brought these devastations upon us were due to the influence of the "uneducated populace." The alignment is not that of the classes who have gone through our universities on the one side and those who have had no better chance than that of the common schools on the other. Although bankers and technically trained economists saw the issues of debts and reparations more clearly than the general public, we must keep in mind the larger fact that the governments which drifted to war both in 1914 and in 1939 were for the most part made up from the most highly educated classes. The diplomacy which led to both wars had been in the hands of highly educated men; the policies which led to the almost complete destruction of the capitalist system were policies imposed by educated capitalists themselves.

The European governments which in the postwar years drifted to economic chaos were bourgeois governments drawn from the "capitalist class." The result of their management of things was to destroy the security of their order. Outside the specialists they were as blind to elementary economic truth as the rest of the nation.

All of Us Are the People, and All Fallible

But note the difficulty of any honest discussion of this problem of how to avoid past errors if one accept the premise that the "people" are not the public as a whole, but that on the one side are down-trodden masses "whose voice is the voice of God," of infallible judgment that is; and on the other, evil and rapacious exploiters whose antisocial interests are responsible for whatever errors the nations may commit. To suggest that the one effective remedy is an educational treatment which will expose popular fallacy and unveil illusion, is to expose oneself to charges of antidemocratic bias, of semi-Fascism. The implication seems to be that you are "blaming the people" instead of the oppressors. To suggest that a banker or a stockbroker can be as big a fool in politics as a plumber or a teamster is, it would seem, to side with the banker against the teamster, to side with privilege against the oppressed.

If, however, we brush aside these absurdities, and recognize what is, today at least, broadly the truth, that we are all of us "the people"; that our society has become so much a bourgeois society in the mass as to have made the century-old Marxist conception of a rigid class structure out of date and untrue, then, in that case we need no longer maintain the pretense that *we* can do no wrong, that *we* are infallible, that *our* voice is the voice of God. We can afford to be honest with ourselves, and show a little decent humility in recognizing that we are perfectly capable of mistakes, lazinesses, prejudices, animosities, partisanships, and that the only hope of being relatively right is to face these facts, to admit them as part of our common human nature, and to be on the lookout for them; to take note of those psychological shoals and rocks upon which we may go shipwreck if we do not face their existence.

One commonly felt objection to telling John Citizen that much of his misery is due to his own indifference about his job of citizenship, is the idea that he will lose his moral indignation, his aggressive energy to destroy privilege, unless he has a definite, imaginable enemy to fight—"the Fascist," "the capitalist," "the imperialist." But the experience of the last twenty years shows that the Fascist himself can turn this tendency to better account than the democrat can. The exploitation of suspicion and animosity, the creation of scapegoats, has worked far more against freedom than for it, in Germany as elsewhere.

Indeed, as we have seen, that particular form of exploitation has been one of the main instruments in the hands of the Hitlers, whether they used it to separate a France from a Britain, or the nations of the West from Russia; or to create internal divisions, as within France, in the period immediately preceding the war. It is time that we, the people, realized that freedom depends now far more upon the capacity for co-operation between differing groups than upon the readiness of one group to fight another.

This Is Our War: the People's

For this is the people's war in a very simple and obvious way. If the Nazis and their allies succeed, the mass of men everywhere will be governed by a small oligarchy or feudal order, whose "law" would be simply their commands, the governed having little or nothing to say about it. Nor would Nazi ruthlessness be qualified by any Christian tradition of chivalry or mercy. For the Nazis stand for a system of morals and government from which the ethic of mercy and chivalry is quite consciously and of set purpose excluded.

The core of their governing organization, already elaborate and far-reaching, would be a self-perpetuating closed party. It would own the state—all states—operating an inquisition, the Gestapo, both more efficient and more ruthless than the inquisitions of old; using terror, torture, vast killings on the Polish and Czechoslovakian scale, with an omnipresent secret police. The world would be under the rule of this new Satanic Vatican, irresponsible, self-perpetuating, dictating to the common man in every aspect of his life; so that none could call his life or his soul his own.

A few years ago the idea that such a thing was within the realm of possibility, that a tiny minority could thus impose its authority on the vast majority, would have seemed utterly unreal, fantastic, quite impossible. But we know today, in the light of tragic experience, that it is not impossible, not fantastic, and that on a very large scale it has actually been carried out. If once established, it would not be easy to overthrow, because technology provides today means whereby a small central body of men can maintain repression and terror more completely over a far wider area than has ever been possible in history before. The new political inquisition will be more efficient, more effective in controlling men than the inquisitions of old because of the nature of the instruments the minority could use. In the old days, men could take refuge in the forests and in the wilds, escape to new lands in their flight from oppression. Today there are no forests and no wilds that the Gestapo of the Nazi party, equipped with radio, airplane, submarine, tank, bomb, cannot reach. Revolution is rendered infinitely harder. In the old days the arms of the revolutionary were pikes or bows and arrows, a battle-ax; later a primitive firearm, all within the capacity of the peasant himself or a good blacksmith to manufacture. But the airplane, the thousand-pound bomb, the tank, the equipment wherewith to meet a panzer division—these things cannot be made secretly and hidden in the mountains by the solitary revolutionary.

Even when the advantage was much more on the side of sheer numbers than it is in these days of machines, the slave state of old lasted a long, long time. Slave societies, like those which built the pyramids, were exceedingly stable. The power of the priest-kings of Egypt lasted thousands of years. The minds, as well as the bodies, of the slaves bowed to the power of the ruler.

And, just as the very complexity of the physical instruments of our time give the advantage to the governing few as against the mass, to any group that succeeds in seizing power, so, similarly, do those instruments by which we control the minds of men—printing, the newspapers, the radio—give power for perpetuating a moral enslavement. In the Nazi state the children are very scientifically "conditioned," not merely to accept their slavery, but to glory in it, to be ready to die for it; for the Fuehrer whose word is its law.

What We Must Pay for Freedom

We have seen how this tiny minority of evil men has imposed its power so far. It has imposed it by applying, with a thoroughness and to a degree unknown before, the most ancient device of tyranny —divide and conquer. The people, the great masses, have been an easy prey because they were so easily divided—divided by their nationalism into a large number of relatively small political groups; divided even within those groups by social and political doctrines. So divided were they that they could not in fact agree on what they wanted, or—which is to say almost the same thing when it comes to unified action—what they wanted most and first; what purposes should be put in the forefront of their effort; what minor purposes they were prepared to sacrifice or postpone for their major purposes.

We know one purpose they all decided to put first—the independence and freedom, each of his own nation-state; the right to manage their national affairs without any reference at all to the effect of what they did in the way of tariffs or armaments or monetary regulation on the fate of others. They insisted upon acting with complete independence, with no obligations of any kind so far as other states were concerned: freedom was to be absolute, untrammeled, unqualified.

Of that decision we can say with certainty three things. First: that it was an extremely popular decision, so popular that the very words that gathered about it—freedom, independence—became hallowed words, capable of deeply moving men, moving them more deeply, perhaps, to political action than any other words whatsoever.

And the second thing which we can say of this demand for complete, absolute independence and freedom is this: that it represents an aim completely impossible of fulfillment, for the simple reason that absolute freedom for one, means in the world in which we happen to be living destruction of the freedom of another. "Where all demand complete freedom, none in the end has any."

And the third thing that we can say of it, with complete assurance, is that it is precisely this kind of claim, made by each nation, that has delivered nearly all the nations of Europe over to the mercy of Hitler and threatens now to deliver the world.

The largest possible measure of freedom and independence for men and nations can only be secured by co-operation, and co-operation means that each accepts obligations to the others, undertakes to do certain things and to refrain from doing certain other things. Without the assumption of these obligations and this responsibility, which limit the freedom of each, there can in the end be no real freedom at all; and there will quite certainly ultimately be subservience to violence.

This truth is seldom told to John Citizen and a good deal of trouble is taken to hide it from him—to pretend that it is not a truth. Let us see in what way this is the case.

Whenever, these last years, it was suggested to (for instance) the English John Citizen that the fulfillment of these obligations was the price of his freedom and security, the demagogues of the Right were able to persuade him that far from having any obligation to the foreigner, the foreigner was the main cause of the trouble, and should be vigorously excluded from the country and the Empire, his goods kept out by high tariffs, his people by exclusion laws. The demagogue of the Left too often tried to persuade John that freedom could be defended best, not by the fulfillment of obligations in the international field, but by the destruction of the capitalist at home, thus making social reform the enemy of that political security in the world by which alone socialism (as Russia is now learning) can be defended from destruction by external violence.

Even now there is a tendency to represent freedom as something to be achieved, not as the result of human co-operations, but as the result of destroying some enemy class within the nation.

The Fascination of the Scapegoat

Some of the reasons for the failure of the European states to hang together so as to make it impossible for a Hitler to apply the "simple and deadly plan of one by one" are obvious enough. Hanging together means accepting certain obligations, including the obligation to fight for others in order that, in their turn, they shall be ready to fight for you. But the politician who insists that to have peace and security we must assume obligations, fulfill duties, is at a disadvantage (in appealing to a possibly bored and half-interested electorate), as compared with the politician who insists that the way to get peace is to have no obligations at all, to give no undertakings, to refuse to become entangled in commitments, "to mind your own business and let others mind theirs." Senator Lodge knew this fact better than President Wilson. In economics there is a law known as the Gresham Law: when debased coins circulate side by side with good, the good tend to disappear because the public keep the good when they can, and pass on the bad, which therefore remain in circulation. There is some similar Gresham Law operative in public opinion.

But there is something more.

To the fact that Wilson's method involves a duty, an obligation, and isolationism does not, has to be added the fact that the isolationist, almost everywhere, is able to provide a further factor of popularity in the shape of a devil, a scapegoat upon whom to blame the phenomenon of war. If it can be shown that war instead of being caused by the international anarchy, the ending of which would involve some obligation on everyone's part, is caused instead by wicked villains—international bankers, financiers, armament makers, Jews, British imperialists—whom we can belabor and upon whom we can blame our troubles, there is not only escape from the burden of obligations, there is escape into entertainment. For, as every movie scenario writer knows, to provide a truly wicked villain whom "you will love to hate" (as the advertisement of one movie put it) is to provide an essential element of drama, particularly the type of drama into which so many like to escape. We can indeed only explain the universality of such phenomena as anti-Semitism (remembering that there are tens of thousands of anti-Semites who have never seen a Jew, never in any way suffered at the hands of a Jew) by the fact that men do need to have some villain, some devil to hate in politics. (Hitler knew that so extremely well.) The Jew is a good receptacle for the necessary outlet of this emotion, because he is everywhere slightly foreign. That is an additional attraction. For if there is a deep-rooted tendency in men to try to find a scapegoat upon whom to blame our troubles, there is a further tendency to distrust and fear those outside the herd or tribe, whether the herd or tribe be nation, class, club, church, or school.

All these impulses converged in the years which followed the last war to make foreign policy isolationist, not only in Britain and America but in Russia, Ireland, and other countries as well. The isolationism in the case of America was sustained and strengthened by those groups of intellectuals who caught the Marxist fashion (there are fashions in ideas as much as in women's hats), a fashion now rapidly declining. For some years the nationalists and isolationists availed themselves of Marxist interpretations in ascribing the drift to war, not to the absence of any international political society, to the prevailing political anarchy in the foreign field, but to the machinations of the capitalists and rather particularly, in America, to the British imperialists.

In the United States, for the best part of twenty years, nearly all explanation of war has centered upon the offenses of Europeans and alleged confederates in this country; the shortcomings of the Versailles Treaty, British imperialism, the armament makers, the bankers, the foreign bond holders, Wall Street, the Morgans. It has all been expressed in a vast political literature every addition to which did but make stronger in the mind of John Citizen (so far as he was affected directly, or directed, by all this writing) the conviction that this country's entrance into the last war had been a vast error (a Gallup poll revealed at one period an 80 per cent majority for the view that the participation of the United States in the war had been a mistake); that he had been swindled by British propaganda; that the country he had helped had welshed on its just debts and left the American tax payer burdened with them; that the bankers had been in cahoots with the armament makers to produce the war to the end that they might make profits; that Wall Street was in league with the British aristocracy to make this country the sucker; that the League was a British invention devised for the purpose once more of entrapping this country into the support of British interests; that Germany had had a raw deal; that there could never be peace in the world while Britain owned a quarter of it; that Germany, Italy, and Japan were Have-not nations that had been denied their fair share of the wealth of the world; that if Britain could be made to disgorge some of the loot she had stolen in a long and shameful career of piracy, the ends of fair play, peace, and justice would be served.

It is already a little difficult for Americans, now in the first year of the Second World War, to recall that that was in very truth the mood and matter of book after book which appeared in the two decades following the last war, and was a daily indoctrination in much of the popular press. At one stage in the development of this mood, [8] books were written to prove that the economic competition between America and Britain made war between them all but inevitable, if not inevitable; and that, in any case, the one supreme purpose of American policy should be to avoid entanglement in the purposes of Britain or in the "never-ending quarrels of Europe." A whole long list of historians, writers, journalists, commentators—including such names as Charles Beard, Harry Elmer Barnes, Judge

---

[8] The mood, however, finds expression as late as 1940. In Theodore Dreiser's book *America Is Worth Saving* (Modern Age Books) occur very many passages —running to page after page—like the following:

Weren't we "Uncle Shylocks" when we timidly asked the English for our money back? Or don't you remember? How dared we expect His Majesty, Defender of the Faith, personal representative on earth of the Deity and exponent of civilization as well as the good and the beautiful here below, to bother himself about a little matter of squaring a debt of honor? And His Majesty with his imperial hands full defending the sacred principle of Democracy, which barbarians (an English word for anyone who tries to imitate England) were threatening all over the place! To defend this holy thing was the most delicate of tasks requiring full concentration and no noisy interruptions from across the Atlantic. The barbarians had to be made just strong enough to enslave their own people and a few other miscellaneous "peoples of whom we know nothing" (Chamberlain's reference to the Czechs), while yet not being allowed to get out of hand and infringe on England's enslaving prerogatives in the "Commonwealth of Nations."

Bausman, Quincy Howe, Theodore Dreiser, Ludwell Denny, Upton Close—made their contribution to this profound conviction of the public mind which expressed itself in repudiation of the League, the Court, in isolationalism; in such legislation as the Neutrality Act and the Johnson Act.

Is Clarification of Foreign Policy Possible?

It is sometimes argued—and still more often implied—that the issues behind a war like this cannot be reduced to such simple terms as to be grasped by the nonexpert; that all simplification, or even clarification, is distortion and ought not to be attempted.

This book rejects such a proposition. To know a few fundamental truths about the working of human society—which are commonly simple truths—so well as to be able almost unconsciously to test policy in the light of them, is a better foundation for good political judgment than a confused and uncertain grasp of a great many facts. It is truer perhaps of international politics than of most departments of knowledge to say that it is possible to "know everything and understand nothing."

Moreover, foreign policy, international affairs, are commonly regarded as things in which the experts differ violently, one professor of the subject like Woodrow Wilson (a college professor of political science and the author of books on the subject, as well as a politician) presenting proposals regarded by other students of the subject as absurd and mischievous. The voter sees rival schools of thought standing by mutually exclusive notions. One school holds "power politics" to be an evil in themselves; another school insists that all politics are power politics, in that all politics involve the use of power. One school urges that peace must be based upon a Balance of Power, another that the Balance must be transformed into a Concert, or Community of Power. One school favors federation as against a League; another one wants a merely consultative League; another a League with teeth; another favors regional federations as against wider instruments. We hear much of pan-Americanism, of

Anglo-Saxonism—all related to intricate problems of sea and air power, economic resources, self-sufficiency, racial conflicts, relations of East and West, China, India, Sovietism, international finance and capitalism; the literature of it is enormous, complex, contradictory.

For John Citizen, the net result of it all is apt to be hopeless confusion. How, with his limited leisure, his pressing day-to-day preoccupations of a personal kind, is he to pass upon and pronounce judgment on these vast complexities which baffle even the professors?

Yet he is compelled in the last resort to pronounce judgment; and does so commonly in no uncertain terms. There are occasions (as in the "khaki" election of 1918 in Britain) when he does not hesitate to indicate a policy to a prime minister or, on this side of the Atlantic, to destroy a Wilson, reject a League, pass a Neutrality Act, insist on debt payments, raise tariffs which may make the payments impossible, or so affect the welfare of foreign nations and the course of events throughout the world as finally to engulf John Citizen himself in their repercussions.

It is plain therefore that the citizen's puzzlement and confusion do not usually result in a decision on his part to "leave it to the experts." Indeed, if he did so decide, he would still have to decide which expert, in view of the fact that the experts so often contradict each other. Nor, in fact, does he, in the democracies at least, "leave it to the government." If democracy means anything at all, it is for him—and for him alone in the very grave issues—to decide his fate, his "way of life," the kind of world in which he wants to live; to let government know what he wants.

Nor do the decisions which he is compelled to make just now bear merely or mainly upon the postwar settlements, or the New Order. His views, very vocally and dogmatically expressed of late in Britain, on such matters as the Second Front, can certainly have bearing upon the actual strategy of a war—as some of the public statements of Mr. Churchill have made abundantly plain.

The very first condition of helping John to become master of his fate, of enabling him to avoid a Third World War, is to induce him to face fully the fact that wars are not in the last analysis made by governments, capitalists, financiers or armament makers. On the contrary, wars are made by the ordinary man acquiescing for a variety of reasons in policies the intention of which is usually peace, and the result of which is, too often, war. Those policies may suit the ends of predatory governments, capitalist financiers, armament makers, as little intending war as John himself. It is John's ideas on such things as the proper methods of national defense; his feeling about nationalism, internationalism, patriotism, religion, morality, of what is important and what unimportant, what permissible and what not, that govern the course of policy and so determine war or peace, determine indeed the kind of world in which we live. By reason mainly of that nationalism by which he swears, and which has split Europe into nations so isolationist that they were incapable of co-operation for defense, war has come upon us. But as he has changed the object of his loyalties and passions many times in the past, it is unlikely that we have seen the last change. Whether he changes to a worse or a better loyalty will depend upon the degree of his understanding of the basic processes of his society. That men should fight is perhaps part of our nature; but what we fight about is part of our nurture, education, way of thought; the way we see things.

In facing the problem of education in the technical sense, as preparation for the future, we should face above all this devastating fact: the most learned generation the world has ever known seems to be in a fair way of proving itself the most foolish and cruel, the most destructive of its own happiness. Never before in history have men had at their disposal so much accumulated knowledge, so many records, libraries, books, encyclopedias, card indices, newspapers, schools, colleges, universities, lectures, lecturers, teachers, professors; never before in history have men possessed such amazing instruments (for example, the radio) for the exchange of information and ideas. Never before has nation been able to speak to nation, instantaneously across the width of the earth, as nations can speak today.

Yet as the result of it all men seem less capable of managing their society than they were twenty-five hundred years ago, in, say, Athens, which had very few books indeed and no newspapers, no radios, no printing, and twenty-five hundred years' less of accumulated knowledge than we have. Today, Germany, the most learned nation of the world, the most scholastically drilled, possessing proportionately more professors and teachers than any other, is precisely the nation which assuredly has shown itself politically the least wise, which has delivered itself over to the guidance of dangerous fanatics; and has turned its whole educational apparatus into an instrument for promulgating doctrines, many of which educated men—including those who teach them—know to be wicked nonsense.

Nor is that all. If one examine certain of the major errors committed by governments and peoples this last twenty years, one is obliged to confess that a very modest degree of wisdom, demanding no special knowledge, would have sufficed to prevent the commission of those errors; as the next chapter will attempt to show.

So we get back to an earlier proposition:

If the world has nearly destroyed itself, it is not from lack of knowledge in the sense that we lack the knowledge, say, to release atomic energy (incidentally, a piece of knowledge which would probably finish off civilized mankind), but it is due to the fact that the mass of men have not applied to public policy knowledge which they already possess, which is indeed of almost universal possession, deducible from the facts of everyday life.

If this is true—and it seems inescapable—then no education which consists mainly in the dissemination of "knowledge" can save us. If men can disregard in their policies the facts they already know, they can just as easily disregard new facts which they do not at present know. What is needed is the development in men of that particular type of skill which will enable them to make social use of knowledge already in their possession; enable them to apply simple, sometimes self-evident, truths to the guidance of policy.

Let us summarize the conclusions of this chapter.

(1) The supreme factor in the shaping of our society, in achieving freedom and happiness, is the quality of the public mind, the quality

of the common people's political judgment. No effective policy of victory or of stable peace can be successfully pursued, whatever the particular plan, blueprint, constitution, if the mass of the public are unconvinced, confused, divided on the simplest and most fundamental principles of security, peace, and plenty. While a grasp of the simpler social truths (like the co-operative nature of defense against the violence of minorities) is not of itself sufficient to solve all public problems, that understanding is indispensable to the solution of any; and the lack of it may constitute, and repeatedly has constituted in the recent past, a complete barrier to the achievement of the people's purposes; a complete frustration of the people's intention.

(2) If judgment goes wrong when the facts necessary for sound judgment are easily available, it is commonly because impulses within us, partisanships, tempers, irritations, hostilities, pugnacities, vanities, the disposition to think with our blood (which the Nazis deem desirable) have been inadequately guided or disciplined by our education for civilization: that civilization against which there is a constant tendency for men to revolt. It is now, after the event, clear that the rejection of policies demanded by peace and security was due, in part at least, to the emotions and passions which gather about nationalism; to ideological and doctrinal conflicts like those which marked the wars of religion and today mark social and economic ideologies; such rivalries as those of Protestant and Catholic in Ireland, Jew and Arab in Palestine, Hindu and Moslem in India, and the innumerable tribal feuds of the Balkans; and to the deep desire of each to dominate the other. These conflicts are no more "inevitable" than panic in a theater is inevitable when a fire alarm is sounded; or panic in a shipwreck. A foreknowledge of our tendencies helps us to discipline them.

(3) The political power achieved by demagogues like Hitler or the Japanese militarists is more dangerous and damaging to human welfare and freedom than the economic power of capitalism, which in any case is being brought more and more under public, collective control and direction; a process which must be continued. Events

have proved that, while the Hitlers or the militarists can control the capitalists (by the simple device of imprisoning, exiling or executing them), the capitalists cannot control the Hitlers.

(4) In so far as vested interests have retained their power to exploit the public, it has been because of the relative ease with which the people—whether we think of the people as non-German Europe or as the population of a single country like France, or China, or India, or in some respects the United States—can be divided, one section persuaded that its special interest as against another section is more vital than the general interest common to both; and because it is so much easier to stir emotions, particularly those rooted in instinctive hostilities—nationalistic, group, or religious—than to secure rational judgments, even those of enlightened self-interest. The most dangerous vested interests are more likely to be demagogic politicians seeking power, co-operating with newspapers seeking circulation, than they are to be economic pressure groups as usually understood.

(5) The understanding of the more fundamental social principles, without which nothing stable can be built, is usually quite within the competence of the ordinary citizen and voter, without specialist knowledge or elaborate academic learning. The present miseries of the world are not due to lack of "book learning," but lack of better understanding of the great commonplaces of human association. (The Abraham Lincolns have been politically wiser than the professors.) The task of formal education should be mainly to develop the skills by which the commonplace truths of everyday life can be used as a guide in the control of public policy.

The central truth which, used as a guide of policy, might have saved the world from a Second World War, is in itself simple; and though no panacea, insufficient of itself to save us, is indispensable; there can be no salvation unless we do understand it. It is often difficult of practical application; which is why widespread comprehension of it is so important.

CHAPTER III

The Key

THE purpose of this book is to help the average busy citizen, professing no expert knowledge of foreign affairs, to play the most effective part possible in the shaping of policy for the winning of the war, and, afterward, in the right use of victory; so that there will not be a Third World War twenty years hence, as this war follows that of a little more than twenty years ago.

It is true that the normal citizen has already a passionate desire to win the war and to prevent its repetition, when his children would be the victims—as the children of the men who fought in the last war are now the victims of the present one. But the history of the last quarter of a century proves, with tragic emphasis, that the clearest will and intention may be defeated by misunderstanding of the policies necessary to make the will effective, and to realize the intention.

For twenty years the average citizen of the democracies, of which America is the chief, has not merely had the intention to avoid this Second World War; he has been moved by an almost savage determination never again to be drawn into wars waged outside his frontiers. It was within his power, as we shall see, to have given effect to both decisions. Yet, contrary to his intention, fixed and strong, the Second World War has come and engulfed him. His will, intention, determination—and power—have all been completely defeated.

In the pages which follow an attempt is made to show that the explanation is to be found in the disregard of certain quite elementary truths which lie at the root of all organized society; that the mistakes of policy which have led to the Second World War stem mainly from one central misconception concerning the indispensable condition of peace, and that a clearer perception of this main principle provides the best means by which the preoccupied layman can avoid the chief mistakes of policy of the past.

In every European democracy today certain truths are accepted as so obvious and self-evident as not to be worth discussion. The patriot in France, for instance, agrees that France's liberation and future security are dependent upon her co-operation with Britain and other nations also menaced by Hitler. The lesser states of the continent know perfectly well that their liberation and future security depend upon hanging together, upon unity; the Englishman knows that to help China or Russia is to help Britain defend herself; that if by some means China could in the next few months push back the Japanese armies, and the Russians push back the Germans, then every British city, as a direct consequence, would sleep more soundly with diminished risks of bombardment. All this is so evident to the average Englishman today that you would merely irritate him by dwelling upon it. Why labor the obvious? But this thing, today so obvious, was yesterday—a few years ago only—hotly denied. The suggestion which some did make in 1932 that Britain had an interest in helping China to defend herself, or three years later the same kind of interest in helping Ethiopia, or later Spain, or later Czechoslovakia, did not then seem an expression of the obvious; it seemed to very many the expression of arrant nonsense, of dangerous warmongering. What earthly interest could Britain have in an obscure quarrel on the other side of the earth? What concern was the fate of Ethiopians or Czechs to us?

Yet if the truth which all see today could have been seen a little earlier, the probability is that the world would not now be at war. Or, to put the point a little more fully we can say this:

> If those in the democracies who did see the truth early had been more numerous, and if those who saw it late had done so a bit earlier, war would either have been prevented, or would have presented us with far less of peril.

Note certain implications of this last proposition. In the field of ideas (which are, as we have already seen, the foundation of action) as in the military field, the day is sometimes won by a very small margin. The vote of a dozen senators, in rejecting American participation in the League, set America's course of foreign policy for several crucial years in one direction instead of another; the vote of the French Cabinet which decided upon surrender instead of continuing the war from Algiers was very close. If two or three (and several, we know, were in a state of deep indecision) had voted the other way, it is fair to say that none of North Africa today would be in Italian or German hands, the French Fleet would be fighting on the Allied side, Dakar would be an Allied outpost, Indo-China would not have been yielded to Japan, whose conquests would then have been much more difficult. The outlook would be very different indeed from what it is.

I call attention to the narrowness of margin in opinion which separated one policy from another, because it bears very directly upon the worthwhileness of educational effort of the right kind. It is, of course, to be expected that, despite every effort education may make toward clarifying public opinion, many political follies will remain uncorrected, many problems unsolved. That is not the point. If our efforts result in only relatively slight improvement in policy at certain strategic points, that slight improvement may conceivably make the difference, so far as democracy is concerned, between slavery and freedom, life and death.

Why did John reject yesterday what he accepts so readily today? The main facts by which he now judges were as available to him when he rejected this policy as they are now when he accepts it. They are not facts of technical nature. They have been pointed out repeatedly, incessantly, by certain minorities of the public, alike in Britain and America, and by certain political leaders and writers. They formed the subject, especially in Britain, of prolonged political debate. But the dominant majority, the voting majority, ignored the facts, or refused to draw from them the conclusions they now draw. Among other reasons for such refusal is that the conclusion now drawn, compelled by events, happens to constitute the kind of truth which obscure psychological forces within ourselves tempt *so* many of us to ignore until visible and imminent peril enforces recognition. Not merely were the vital facts as available when we rejected the policy as when later we accepted it (the "we" being the dominant majority), but the very arguments we now regard as platitudinous we earlier regarded as nonsense.

This, surely, is one of the primary factors, if not the ultimate one, in the whole vast episode of the Second World War. If we allow it to go unexamined, the forces which produced that particular blindness in the past will almost certainly—perhaps at some moment of grievous peril in the strategy or conduct of the war—produce similar blindness again and precipitate us into other disastrous and, it may be, this time, irreparable error.

There is a very great tendency to let that primary question of why today's obviousness was yesterday so obscure, go unexamined, on the general principle that it belongs to the past and that it is no good crying over spilled milk. Which constitutes a very dangerous complacency indeed. For it is only by understanding why we made certain mistakes in the past that we can hope to avoid their repetition in the future.

It is not true—as is sometimes averred—that our peoples are complacent or half-hearted in their war effort; unwilling to make the necessary sacrifices for victory. It is true, however, that we pass far too lightly over our major errors of past policy, tend to wipe consideration of them from our minds, with the result that we are entirely capable of repeating them all over again.

The Basic Principle

What then is the kind of fact, now so visible, that we previously ignored? What principle of policy which we now recognize as obviously wise, did we yesterday so disastrously reject as obviously absurd?

It is this exceedingly simple and basic social principle: unless the community—whether it be a community of persons or of states —is prepared to use its combined power for the defense of the individual member who is made the victim of lawless violence, there can be neither law, nor peace, nor justice, nor stable civilization. The attempt to make those things compatible with the rule that each shall defend himself by his own power must, on the face of it, fail. For by that rule, each to be secure must be stronger than his neighbor, who is then deprived of security. Each cannot be stronger than the other. Where each is his own sole defender the whole community is exposed to the risk of domination by any violent minority that can make itself stronger than any single individual.

There are a multitude of forms in which this social principle can be stated. But perhaps the form which relates it most immediately to the coming of the present war (and to the present Allied strategy) is this:

No nation in the modern world can possibly defend itself effectively against the form of violence most likely to threaten it unless it is prepared to take its part in the defense of others. By refusing to concern ourselves with the defense of others we make our own impossible.

Does anyone deny this proposition today? It is only necessary to examine the position of any and every one of the nations threatened or overcome by the Axis to see that, in the light of the event, the proposition is undeniable. What would be the chances of Russian success, of recovery of the immense Russian areas which the German army now holds, if America and Britain withdrew from the war, made peace with Germany, and refused all material to Russia? What would be the position of China if America and Britain withdrew all help to the Chinese and made peace with Japan? Of the British Empire, if America and Russia made peace with the Axis and disinterested themselves in the fate of Britain? What of France, if peace were now made? And those are the great powers of the world. In the case of the lesser states the truth that none can defend itself merely by its own strength is more obvious still.

It is, on the face of it, clear that, if each of a score of nations says:

"We will defend only ourselves, when our own soil has been invaded; we will accept no obligation to defend others," then they are all at the mercy of a gang or combination that can make itself stronger than any one of the twenty, because in that case such a gang can do what Hitler has done—destroy them in detail, beginning with the lesser (Austria, Czechoslovakia, Norway) so as to use their resources or strategic position as added power for attack upon the next victim. It is clear on the face of it that a Norway or a Belgium could not possibly defend itself single-handed against a Germany of seventy or eighty million; as it is perfectly clear that a France or a Britain could not defend itself if it watched with neutral indifference the swallowing one by one of a number of lesser states whose resources would be added to those available to the aggressor for later attacks. As little could a United States effectively defend itself if it had allowed a Britain to be conquered by a Germany; and a China and an India by a Japan.

That surely is the lesson of Europe. These states of continental Europe have perished as free nations because each said in effect: "We refuse to be concerned in defending the security of the rights of others; we will defend only our own." Because all said this in one form or another, they were all at Hitler's mercy; at his mercy however much they armed. A Norway or a Denmark might devote 90 per cent of all its national resources to arms and still be at his mercy. The more these democracies armed while refusing to co-operate for mutual defense, the better were the Nazis pleased; for they knew that, given this one condition of separate and individual defense, the arms they piled up would by their inevitable conquest become instruments of Nazi power. The splendid armaments of Czechoslovakia, the great arsenal of the Skoda works, became part of the armament of Germany without the firing of a single shot because the men of Munich had for years made their slogan: "We will not defend others, only ourselves." The slogan had eaten into the heart of France where so many had said not merely, "Why should we fight for the Czechs?" but also, "Why should we fight for the English?" It had eaten into the heart of many English, who, years before, had said, "Why should we fight for the Manchurians, or the Chinese, or the Abyssinians, or the Spanish Republicans, or for Danzig or the Rhineland?" From the moment that Hitler could get those whom he planned to conquer to be guided by such slogans, he knew full well that they would be at his mercy, for he could pick them off one by one, applying the most hackneyed device of conquest and tyranny: divide and rule.

After all, ten men *can* overcome a hundred, ten times their number, if the hundred insist that each must defend himself individually, not in co-operation with the others; for in that case the ten do not face a hundred, they only face one, one at a time. Thus, less than two hundred million in Germany and Japan threaten two thousand million throughout the world at large. The menace to the peoples of the world comes from a tenth of their number. That is the strategic or mathematical statement of the truth we have all forgotten or repudiated. But one can formulate it also in the moral form already indicated: If we will not defend the vital rights of others, then inevitably we reach a situation in which it becomes impossible to defend our own.

Now, I do insist that we are here confronting a fact self-evident and undeniable. Is it, or is it not, true that it is clearly impossible for a Norway to defend herself by her own power against a Germany? Or for a Denmark so to do, or a Belgium, a Holland, or a Czechoslovakia, or for that matter a France, or, as we are now learning, a Britain? Amongst so much that is obscure, doubtful, uncertain, we have something here which is quite certain, quite undeniable. Indeed we now—America, Britain, Russia, China, and twenty-four other united nations—no longer deny it; we act upon it. We know now that the defense of Greece is part of America's defense; the defense of China part of Britain's defense; the defense of Yugoslavia a part of the defense of China.

If I were to elaborate that truth at any length the reader would find it platitudinous, and tiresome. John the garage hand as much as the professor would agree upon its obviousness. But, once more, this thing we thus deem obvious was denied by most of us—denied with anger and contempt as theoretic nonsense—only a year or two ago, and in the case of some of us only a few months ago—until, that is, December 7, 1941. In recent years it has been denied alike by British, Americans, French, Danes, Dutch, Norwegians, Greeks, Poles, Yugoslavs. . . .

It will be said perhaps that the facts were not previously available for the judgments we now draw; that the world could not foresee the power of aggression which Germany and Japan have developed. But the peculiarity of the situation which we now face was always inherent in that method of anarchy in the international field which we have always insisted upon perpetuating. So little is it true that this development could not have been foreseen, that for years a minority—a somewhat despised minority—has insisted that the perils we now confront would quite inevitably arise in lesser or greater degree unless we faced the meaning of the obvious fact which we seemed determined to ignore.

Even before the end of the last world war the essential fact was obvious enough. In a book which appeared in May, 1918, occurred this passage:

The survival of the Western Democracies, in so far as that it is a matter of the effective use of their force depends upon their capacity to use it as a unit, during the war and after. That unity we have not attained, even for the purposes of the war, because we have refused to recognize its necessary conditions—a kind and degree of democratic internationalism to which current political ideas and feelings are hostile; an internationalism which is not necessary to the enemy, but is to us.

For the Grand Alliance of the Democracies is a heterogeneous collection of nations, not geographically contiguous, but scattered over the world; and not dominated by one preponderant state able to give unity of direction to the group. The enemy alliance, on the other hand, is composed of a group of states, geographically contiguous, dominated politically and militarily by the material power and geographical position of one member who is able by that fact to impose unity of purpose and direction on the whole. If we are to use our power successfully against him in such circumstances, during the war, at the settlement, and afterwards (which may well be necessary), we must achieve a consolidation equally effective. But in our case that consolidation, not being possible by the material predominance of one member, must be achieved by a moral factor, the voluntary co-operation of equals—a democratic internationalism, necessarily based on a unity of moral aim. Because this has not been attained, even during the war, disintegration of our alliance has already set in—involving military cost—and threatens to become still more acute at the peace. The enemy group shows no equivalent disintegration.

No military decision against the unified enemy group can be permanent if at the peace table it becomes evident that the Western Democracies are to revert to the old lack of consolidation, instability of alliance, covert competition for isolated power and territory, and a national particularism which makes common action and co-ordination of power cumbrous, difficult, or impossible. If there is to be a return to the old disunited Western Europe, the parties which among the enemy favour a policy of aggression will realize that, however much their purpose may temporarily be defeated, the greater material unity of their alliance will enable it sooner or later to overcome states which, though superior in the sum of their power, have shown themselves inferior in their capacity to combine it for a common purpose. And that inferiority might arise less from the pressure of any active agent of disruption than from passive hostility to abandoning the old national organisation in Europe, sheer lack of habit and practice in international co-operation, political, military or economic.

. . . This truth is of greater importance to us than the enemy. He can in some measure ignore it. We cannot. His unity, in so far as it rests upon moral factors, can be based upon the old nationalist conceptions; our unity depends upon a revision of them, an enlargement into internationalism.[1]

The writer has here been guilty of the bad taste of quoting from one of his own earlier books. He has done so in order to drive home the point that there was nothing unforeseeable in this present situation; that it was inherent in the world's anarchy even in 1918; that the truth we now recognize but yesterday denied is not a

---

[1] *The Political Conditions of Allied Success*, G. P. Putnam's Sons, New York, 1918.

"new" truth, demanding for its perception elaborate learning and special knowledge; it is a truth which lies at the basis of all organized society and is inherent in the daily life that goes on about us; a truth enunciated in general terms by most of the great religions of the world ("We are members one of another"; "No man can live to himself alone"); terms repeated weekly in our churches. And it is a truth which obviously most people simply did not believe. They did not believe it because they did not understand it. There are some circumstances, once remarked Chief Justice Holmes, in which education in the obvious is far more important than investigation of the obscure.

Let us, therefore, expand a little the enunciation of that truth, which since the last war we have consistently ignored, but upon which we now—after catastrophe—base our policy. It might be stated, in the light of the events unrolling before us, in these terms:

> The basis of all civilization is the defense of each by all; the defense, by the community, of the rights of the individual, beginning of course with the most elementary right of all, the Right to Life, to existence, the right not to be tortured, killed, destroyed. And it has been obvious, at the very least since the last war, that this principle is as true of the relationship of nations as of men.

We recognize this truth in the relationship of persons, within the limits of the nation. Suppose when a person was murdered, the community as a whole said, "Well, after all, it is no affair of ours; it is not our quarrel; let the parties concerned settle it. Why should we expend our taxes on police and courts interfering in the quarrels of others?" If we said that, then there could be no peace, no order, no right, no law, no justice, no civilization. If each man, each household, each political party, each trade-union, each church, each organization had to defend itself by its own power, we know that the whole thing would disintegrate into lawless and bloody violence: into another Dark Age.

A common form of escape from the application of this principle to the relations of states has been to argue that you cannot hale a nation into court and punish it as you can a person. But, of course, in the case of the aggressions of the last twenty years, there was no question of haling a nation to court or punishing it, but of defending a nation the victim of violence. And that we can do, for we are now doing it. We are not discussing here some utopian scheme of world government. We are discussing why we could not have recognized earlier the principle we now recognize and are actually applying in practice.

We should face all the implications of the truth that the present peril of the democracies is explained by the fact that they have repudiated the simplest and most elementary of all those moral truths upon which organized society is based, the one obligation upon which freedom and peace must depend. Events compel the devastating conclusion that the world is now at war because a score or more of nations have during twenty years refused to apply to their relationship the principle which they now apply, and which lies at the root of all organized free society. That principle is extremely simple, undeniable in abstract logic, plainly revealed in the everyday life about us, verified by all human experience. And for twenty years every nation in its relations with others has passionately denied it.

The Moral Miracle

We miss the significance of what is happening unless we realize the importance of distinguishing between two distinct orders of events: those happening in the visible and external world, the actual fall of nations, destruction of states, and the domination or threatened domination of the vast majority of mankind by a relatively small minority, between events of that order and those happening in the minds of men. In this latter sphere we face above all a miracle of blindness. It behooves us therefore not merely to face the facts of yesterday's folly but inquire how it came about that we did not see it to be folly. We are confronted by two miracles, not one: one of a material and another of a moral order. It is the latter which explains the former. Yet it is the mental lapse which we overlook.

I insist upon this "miracle of opinion" because there will be a tendency now to say: "Well, in any case we have seen the facts at last; and it serves no purpose further to labor the point."

But that brings us to another disturbing fact in relation to public opinion. For a very brief period after the last war the public both in Britain and America did see the light; or at least proclaimed very loudly its belief in this primary principle of common restraint of violence; and then suddenly forgot all about it; casually repudiated it, angrily denied it as nonsense. In 1918 the John Citizens everywhere in America were shouting loudly, vehemently, for "a League to Enforce Peace." And, although the principle of co-operation or collective defense just outlined does not need a League in order to give it political expression (there are a hundred ways in which it might be applied to the international situation), a League to Enforce Peace does imply just that principle. The previous chapter has shown how widely accepted was that plan. Yet we know what happened. Within a year or two those who had been most adamant in support of this policy were hounding President Wilson, bitterly opposing his League as a European invention, something which, as one newspaper writer put it, "stank of British propaganda"; (a considerable section of British opinion had opposed the League as "a bit of naïve, unrealistic American uplift") and were shortly to secure its rejection by the Senate.

But if the rejection of the idea of collective defense as the indispensable condition of peace was accomplished more rapidly in America than in Britain, it none the less came about in Britain also, despite a great deal of support for it from informed opinion. By 1935, after Spanish "nonintervention" and the failure of sanctions against Italy, collective defense as a government policy was dead, and was succeeded by the policy of appeasement which led finally to war.

Is the support of the policy we are now pursuing to be as short-lived as soon as the war is over?

It is quite evident that the ready, noisy, unanimous acquiescence in a League to Enforce Peace had no deep roots in understanding. It responded to a mood, a desire, an intention to get rid of war, never to have the tragedy of 1914–1918 repeated. But the roots of understanding and conviction were so shallow that a few blasts of demagogy, the provision of a few convenient scapegoats on which to blame the involvement of the country in the last war, and preoccupation with domestic issues and party politics, suffered to sweep the whole thing away.

Are we to learn by experience? Whether we do or not depends upon our interpretation of experience. Experience does not teach itself, as a glance at the lives of some of your neighbors will suffice to show. Whether or not wisdom comes out of past events depends upon a true reading of them. That justifies a re-examination of the events which led to this Second World War.

We can now be wise after the event and see how we drifted into two wars by misunderstanding the way power must be used to give both defense and peace. To avoid repeating past mistakes we must face the truth about the Versailles Treaty, capitalism, imperialism, nationalism, isolationism, the struggle for power as a means of national self-preservation, and, most important of all, about the confusions of the public mind.

CHAPTER IV

Why the Second War?

A GLANCE through the large body of political literature professing to explain the causes which led to the Second World War
will reveal one predominant theme: Peace failed and the world
was again drifting to war because of the unjust character of the
Versailles Treaty; Germany was strangled economically, deprived of
access to raw materials, her people thereby subjected to intense
social and economic strains . . . It is all very familiar. Particularly
have American opponents of the President's foreign policy dwelt,
since the outbreak of war in 1939, upon the theme that British imperialist policy in 1918 accounted for the Second World War.[1]

Is it open to John Citizen, without special knowledge of history
or of international affairs, to judge the validity of this diagnosis?
Are those facts which are the common knowledge of the average
newspaper reader sufficient to enable him to pass judgment?

This chapter suggests that the answer to these questions is, yes;
that there are certain obvious facts which throw the greatest possible
doubt upon the diagnosis just indicated.

---

[1] During the debate on the Lend-Lease Bill, Senator Clark declared that
"Britain is fighting to retain her hold upon the riches of her Empire—fighting
for precisely the same thing for which she has fought for a thousand years:
commercial supremacy." He went on to declare that as among "German
Nazism, Italian Fascism, Russian Communism, and British Imperialism, there
is little to choose."

Senator Nye was as definite. "The greatest aggressor in all modern history,"
he declared, "has been the British Empire. That Empire," he went on, "is
the despotic, arbitrary, and sometimes tyrannical ruler of almost half a billion
people. It is this Empire which is calling us in the name of democracy."

Senator Holman praised Hitler for "having broken the control of the international bankers and traders over the rewards for the labor of the common
people of Germany." Senator Chandler testified his unwillingness to shed
American blood "in order to allow the British to enslave the people in their
possessions in Bombay and other places."

If the terms of the Versailles Treaty provoked the war of 1939, what provoked the war of 1914? Previous to 1914 Germany possessed her colonies, had the freest kind of access to raw materials of every kind, and, far from being strangled in her trade, was expanding that trade by leaps and bounds. In fact the Germany of 1914 was a Germany of immense and rapidly growing prosperity, with no unemployment as we understand that term today, no considerable popular discontent, and with, incidentally, a large and powerful Social Democratic Party which, on the morrow of war, fully supported that war and the government which made it. Yet the Europe of that Germany—the Europe which was relatively free from insuperable tariff barriers, exchange restrictions, and those aspects of economic nationalism which have since grown up, and which possessed what we should today deem a very liberal economy, drifted to a war which engulfed the whole world.

If we assume the cause of the First World War to be the commercial greed of a Great Britain fearing German commercial competition, then we face a still more uncomfortable fact, namely, that ample territory, access to raw materials, *Lebensraum*, and all the rest of it, is no guarantee against the aggression which leads to war. To assume that the cause on both occasions was indeed to be found in British imperial aggression would at least dispose of the argument that wars arise from the need of Have-not nations for living space, and that we can achieve peace by some sort of territorial redistribution, a better national division of the wealth of the world. For Britain was presumably a Have nation. No territorial redistribution could hope to give others more. If Britain's "possessions" have not satisfied her, what hope is there that others, with greater territories than they now possess, would prove more easily satisfied?

The War and Capitalist Imperialism

Another much canvassed theory of the last twenty years is that the First World War arose as (we are so often told) all wars arise, from the nature of capitalism. They are the result, it is insisted, of the conflict between the various national groups of capitalists struggling with one another for the privileges of investment, trade exploitation, profits. In the decade which followed the last war there were quite a number of books, one by Trotsky and several by Americans, prophesying that these motives would produce a war between Britain and America as the two great trading and industrial countries now that Germany was presumed to be out of the way.

How do the known and very visible events of the last quarter of a century bear on that theory?

The main charge leveled at the British governments of the last ten years is the charge of "appeasement"—appeasement of Japan, of Italy, of Germany. The charge is not that Britain and France were ruthless in defending their capitalist or imperialist interests in China as against assaults by Japan, in North Africa as against the rival empire building by Italy, in Southeastern Europe and Spain as against the thrusts of Germany; the charge is that nothing would persuade the conservative-capitalist government of Britain to risk war in opposing the imperialism of Japan, Germany, and Italy. The theory that wars arise out of the inevitable conflict of rival imperialisms was, in the face of the facts, altered to another theory, namely, that capitalism throughout the world forms a natural if unwritten alliance to oppose popular movements against it. No capitalist government would fight another it was suggested (dog does not eat dog); all would combine to resist any socialist movements. Wars arise, we were seriously told, from the need of capitalism to repress anticapitalist movements.

This is, of course, a far less contradictory theory than the other, far more defensible in logic if one accept the class-war premise. But the facts have nevertheless played havoc with it.

The governments of the German Kaiser and the Austrian Emperor, with which the capitalist allies of 1914 went to war, were not precisely Communist or Socialist or even popular or democratic governments. They, too, were capitalist. And the effect of victory over them was not to improve the position of capitalism in the victor nations, or to check social advance therein. In every one of the belligerent nations, victor and vanquished alike, capitalism (if that describes the economic structure of such countries as the United States, Britain, France) went through strains such as it had not known since the industrial revolution began. In central Europe the millionaire went through the strange experience of finding one morning that his million in the bank would buy one egg but not two. And even in the United States the memory of 1929 is still with us. If the war of 1914 was to strengthen the position of the capitalist, there seems to have been a miscalculation. The stock generalization of the last ten years is that capitalism is on its last legs, finished, done for.

On the other hand the workers, particularly in Britain, have since the last war made very great progress, greater progress in the building up of a system of social security—universal old-age pensions, unemployment insurance, health insurance, child welfare provisions—than had ever been made in any twenty years of British, or any other, history.

Furthermore, those who find in economics—capitalist economics—the standing cause of war, were obliged to reconcile that theory with the fact that, since the last war, the capitalist governments of Britain and France have simply refused to go to war, or to risk it, as against the capitalist governments of Japan and Germany. To explain this pacifist attitude there was invoked a new theory of a world-wide capitalist combination against Socialism, and specifically against Russian Communism. The capitalist states were in fact, we were told, combining to destroy Russia. Thus, the appeasements.

Certain it is that prejudice against and fear of Russia did enter into the appeasement policies. But fear and dislike of Russia were not confined either to capitalists or Conservatives. The British Labour Party and British Trade-Unions distrusted the Communists even more than the Tories did. In the United States we have seen something similar. Large sections of Labor have opposed consistently the Communist "boring from within."

But some of the bitterest opposition to Communism is religious, as the Catholic Hierarchy, and, since the beginning of this war, the Irish part of the Catholic priesthood have made abundantly clear. The Axis has been as ready to war against a Capitalist United States as against a Socialist Russia; a Chamberlainite Conservative British government declared war against the chief member of the Anti-Comintern Pact, at a time when a Communist Russia was that member's quasi-ally; a Conservative Capitalist Churchill warmly welcomed the comradeship in arms of a Communist Russia. These events hardly conform to the Marxist theory that the great struggles of the world are conditioned by the economic rivalry of classes.

A War for National Survival

/ Motives of policy are usually mixed. But if we disentangle the incidental from the primary, fundamental, determining forces, we shall see that the Second World War was not, as much popular theory has insisted, a conflict of rival economic interests in the sense of a "class war." The forecast repeatedly made was that when the war came it would be a war between the rising Communism of Russia and the declining capitalism of the West. Hitlerite Germany (where Nazism had been commonly described by Marxists as "the last throw of capitalism") would either be encouraged to destroy Russia, or actually aid in so doing. We know what became of these forecasts. The war did not arise at all as a conflict between Communism on the one side with capitalism on the other, using Germany as a spearhead. Communist Russia became the quasi-ally of Fascist Germany, which was challenged by the capitalist West. The war arose from motives precisely similar to those which in 1914 prompted the capitalist state of Britain to challenge the equally capitalist state of Germany; not from any motive of defending capitalism or its profits (which obviously the war would, and did, tax so heavily) but from a determination to defend the British state as an independent entity. "Capitalist" Germany on her side showed herself quite ready to make an ally of Communist Russia in order to promote German political power. Russia accepted alliance with

Germany for the purpose of promoting Russian political and military power—the only means the Russian government then believed it possessed of defending the Russian state. In the annexations in the Baltic states and Poland, as in the Finnish war, Communist Russia behaved exactly as capitalist Czarist Russia would have behaved. When Russia attacked Finland and annexed the Baltic states, half of Poland, and Bessarabia, it was not from any economic motive but from motives of military and political security.

Let us stick to facts which now, after the event, are visible enough even if they were not before. Why did Britain in 1914 and the United States two years and some months later, enter the First World War? Why did Britain in 1939 enter the Second World War, and America on the second occasion, also enter it two years and some months after Britain? Neither nation was attacked by Germany on the first occasion. On both occasions Germany would have done a great deal to keep Britain and the United States neutral. During the twenty years that followed the First World War America had taken most elaborate measures to preserve her neutrality and to prevent intervention in "Europe's never-ending quarrels." Public opinion in both countries had been warned abundantly; peace sentiment had become widespread and deep; America, in addition, had developed a bitter sense of having been swindled in the last war; a conviction of having been made the victim of a conscienceless, satanic exploitation for the benefit of unsavory, unavowed, and unavowable vested interests. Resentment against Britain especially was kept alive by a whole library of anti-British books and the influence of powerful newspapers. Yet despite it all— Neutrality Act, Johnson Act, passionate warnings, bitter resentment —here again less than twenty years after the return home of the last American soldiers of World War Number One, American soldiers are once more landing on British soil to fight in another of "Britain's wars," as British Tommies are once more perishing on French soil for the defense of a people whom few Tommies particularly love.

Again, why?

In August, 1914, the British government and people saw what would happen if Russia and France were defeated. They argued:

If Germany wins in this war (1914), conquers Russia, overcomes France, drives to the Channel ports, occupies them, remains there, then Britain will be completely at Germany's mercy, so immense would be German preponderance. In any dispute between ourselves and Germany, Germany would always be the judge, for the simple reason that we should have to yield to her preponderance. We would be in no position to insist even upon our most elementary rights because Germany could dictate to us. She would simply issue the orders and we should simply have to obey. This is a position of defenselessness, of absolute national helplessness, which no free people should be asked to occupy. We refuse to occupy it and we shall fight. We must defend France against invasion because the defense of France is necessary to our own.

Such was the argument of the British in August 1914. Two and a half years later, Americans argued in precisely the same way, taking geographical differences into account, for precisely the same reasons, with precisely the same result as to fighting and challenging German power.

Were the Americans and the British right in thus refusing to allow their nations and people to become subject to the irresponsible and autocratic will of an alien power?

So far they were entirely right.

The Tragic Seesaw

But note what follows. The Allies defeated Germany. Germany now, instead of Britain or France or America, was at the mercy of an alien, outside power, in no position to defend her rights. She occupied, that is, exactly the position which, at an earlier date, Britain and America had argued no free and self-respecting nation should ever be asked to occupy. And by way of proving to Germany that she could safely, and without misgiving, accept that position of inferior power, the Allies imposed upon Germany the Treaty of Versailles, having forbade her in fact even to discuss it. It was imposed in the very palace where forty-eight years previously a victorious Germany had imposed a Treaty upon defeated France. This treaty of 1919 was in fact Versailles Treaty No. 2.

After imposing this Treaty No. 2, Britain and France proceeded to demand vast sums by way of reparation, at the same time notifying Germany that she would not be permitted to increase her export trade; would not be permitted, that is, to obtain the money for payment in the only way in which it could be obtained. Nonfulfillment of the physically impossible conditions was later made ground for invasion of the Ruhr, and indignities of many kinds. There came the appalling inflation in Germany, and later still a period of vast unemployment. It was easy for Germans to blame it all on the Treaty, though in fact the victors were suffering in much the same way. Looking at the Treaty the Germans began to say:

> Well, that is what comes of being weaker than your enemies; of leaving foreigners in such a position that they are able at some moment difficult for you, perhaps, to gang up against you. In order to get justice you must be stronger than your enemies, and you must make it impossible for them to gang up against you. Which means that the only real alternative to being at the mercy of foreigners is to see that foreigners are at your mercy.

And Germany knew it would be quite possible for her to subjugate these foreigners, for she knew that the alliance which had defeated her could not hold together. Its most powerful member had already withdrawn into extreme isolationism. Germany knew that by playing upon the animosities, cupidities, suspicions, hates, of the other nations which composed that alliance, it could be broken up completely; that some of its members could indeed, by the offer of loot (to be taken from a third party) be induced to become Germany's allies.

And so it was. Germany did not really have to break up the alliance which defeated her in 1918. It broke itself up. Two of its chief members became her allies. She was consequently able to take its remaining members, one by one, and defeat them: to annex Austria, to destroy Poland, annexing one half, while Russia took the other half; to destroy France while Russia was still a neutral . . . Very soon Germany had in fact imposed a new treaty of Versailles, Treaty No. 3, and subjected continental Europe to its terms.

Was it a better treaty than the one we wrote in 1918? Will the vanquished accept it? We know that they will not; we know that Germany will be defeated and that Treaty No. 3—the one to which continental Europe is now subjected—will be followed by Treaty No. 4 in which Germany and her allies and satellites will be subjected to conditions even more severe than those of the Treaty of 1919. Of course we believe that, if only we are sufficiently "severe," the next treaty will work; that the guilty this time will be adequately punished and restrained. But the guilty, of course, include not merely Germany but quite a number of nations whose governments have co-operated with Germany: the Italians, the Rumanians, the Bulgarians, the Finns; while there are Slovaks who have fought against the Czechs and many other minorities who, while not liking the Germans, are willing to become their allies, in order to secure redress of national grievances which in their view are infinitely more important than any future peace of the world—just as you have certain Irishmen in Southern Ireland who regard the inclusion of Belfast in their state as an object infinitely more important than the defeat of Hitler, and, in order to achieve what they term "ending of partition," are quite ready to risk the placing of the world in Hitler's hands. It is the nationalist scale of values—and the nationalist logic, for of course, with the defeat of Britain, Ireland too would be in Hitler's hands.

When we talk so casually of knowing better this time how to treat Germany, of the proper severity which is to be meted out to her, of her complete disarmament, we perhaps overlook the fact that such a policy presupposes a capacity of the victors to hang together in its enforcement. If once more we, the victors, hasten to disagree with each other; if each, once more, is to regard his special national claim or grievance as far more important than the solidarity of any international order, then it will be quite impossible to apply the "severe" policy toward Germany—or Japan. If our scale of values, our attitudes and behavior to our allies, are to be after the next victory what they were after the last, then Germany and Japan have merely to bide their time; to detach vital members from our group—next time conceivably a Russia, a China—and the enforcement of the new treaty will become as impossible as, after a year or two, enforcement of the last treaty became.

Britain's participation in the war of 1914-18 was dictated by the motive of survival, which it was hoped to ensure through what is commonly called the Balance of Power policy. That policy was based on the assumption that any power which could completely dominate the continent of Europe could render Britain indefensible; put Britain, that is, in a position in which she would ultimately have to yield to the predominant power—as Czechoslovakia had to yield after Munich.

Critics sometimes make this a charge against Great Britain; accuse her of having involved Britain in war by "playing power politics." [2] Would these critics then have her place herself in a position, or drift into a position, in which the defense of the country would become impossible, and Britain become another Czechoslovakia? The true indictment of the Balance of Power policy is not that under it

---

[2] This is a standing charge made by Germany against Great Britain; was so during the First World War. A London *Times* leading article of March 8, 1915 says:

Our honour and interest would have compelled us to join France and Russia even if Germany had scrupulously respected the rights of her small neighbours and had sought to hack her way through the Eastern Fortresses. The German Chancellor has insisted more than once upon this truth. He has fancied apparently that he was making an argumentative point against us . . . That, like so much more, only shows his complete misunderstanding of our attitude . . . We reverted to our historical policy of the Balance of Power.

Five years later (July 31, 1920) the *Times* makes the same point:

It needed two years of actual warfare to render the British people wholly conscious that they were fighting not a quixotic fight for Belgium and France, but a desperate battle for their own existence.

Britain concerned herself with problems of power throughout the world (any defensive policy necessarily takes into account the way in which power is distributed), but that by its very terms the "balance" of power tends to put power where it does not belong in human society, and where it operates least effectively for the prevention of violence and the defense of right.

Let us see in what way, recalling the outline of the facts just noted, this is so.

Britain and France in 1914, and America later, felt their security placed in jeopardy by prospective German domination. They refused to accept it, or to drift into a position in which they would be at its mercy. As an alternative to the intolerable position of being at the mercy of alien power they proposed that Germany should occupy it, should be at *their* mercy; should accept a position of subordination they had refused to accept. This meant that the attempt to maintain a Balance of Power (what Asquith early in the First World War called "the unstable equilibrium") was bound to result in practice in an oscillation of preponderance of power, first to one side, then to the other. In 1871 the Germans were preponderant, and by that preponderance imposed their settlement upon France. France thereupon proceeded to find allies, first Russia, then England, and finally and temporarily, America, and imposed once more her settlement upon Germany; Germany thereupon proceeded to re-create her preponderance both by building up her own power and by taking advantage of divisions between the Allies, her erstwhile enemies; and of the anarchic and Balkanized condition of so much of Europe. Tomorrow the Allies may once more become preponderant, impose a punitive peace, which would require close and prolonged co-operation between such powers as the United States, Britain, France, Russia, China for its maintenance. Would that co-operation constitute a Balance of Power? Would not Germany, Japan, and Italy be subject to a hostile preponderance of power— and would there be the slightest chance of maintaining peace unless they were?

Balance v. Community of Power

Certainly we do not want a Balance of Power as between the totalitarian states and the democracies, as between aggressors and their victims. We want an overwhelming preponderance of power against the aggressor, and it is doubtful if we can keep that for long if there is a constant effort to maintain a nice "balance" between the Allies themselves. For that would furnish a supreme opportunity for the totalitarians to do once more what they did before—play off one Ally against another, and break up the combination. Our effort must be directed not toward devising a nicely calculated "balance" as between the various Allies, but to finding the common interest behind which the collective power of the whole community of nations may be massed—that common interest being the right of each to life, to self-preservation, to existence free from the menace of lawless violence.

But, it will be asked, will not the sheer fact of Allied predominance present us once more with that precise dilemma previously outlined, in which the dominant party tries to impose the very position it refuses to accept for itself upon the vanquished? Would it not mean a restarting of that old seesaw: the imposition of a domination, a challenge to it, its destruction, followed later by the domination of the other side, in turn challenged and destroyed . . . ?

The answer is that it will, unless, seeing more clearly in the future than we have in the past the true function of power in the maintenance of a free civilization, of peace and order, we make power the instrument of the common interest; so that ultimately, and at a date not too distant, the conquered themselves may join in that purpose and become part of the forces which sustain it. Power can be made, even internationally, an instrument of freedom and justice if we keep clearly before us the nature of the principle or method by which, within the borders of the national community, we do manage to make common power the instrument for the elimination of violence, and the maintenance of some measure of justice.

This does not mean that the principle can always be applied

internationally in its entirety, or ever perhaps applied with complete consistency. Human society and human nature—particularly human nature as operative in international affairs—are too fluid, changing, elusive, for neatly formulated principles to be applied as one might apply a principle of physics to an engineering problem. But one of the advantages of understanding clearly the operation of a social or political method is this: the more clearly we grasp it, the more safely we may at times disregard it and work toward it by indirection.

Arm the Law, not the Litigants

What is wrong in the use of power as we have seen it applied in this seesaw of victory-defeat, defeat-victory, above sketched, Germany imposing her verdict in 1872, France and her Allies in 1918, Germany in 1940, the Allies in . . . ?

That oscillation is the result of using power as the instrument of the rival parties to a conflict, each attempting to make himself judge in his own cause, and of *not* using it as the instrument of a constitution or code under which both parties are prepared to yield the use of force as the instrument of their own verdict in return for certain protections which the code or constitution would afford. Put somewhat differently, one might say that that oscillation, those successive wars, are the result of arming the litigants instead of the law; of refusing to use power as the foundation of a law (however rudimentary that law may be) out of which an international constitution might grow.

For Britain and France in 1918 to take the position: It is intolerable for *us* to be at the mercy of Germany's preponderant power but right for Germany to be at ours, was, obviously, inequitable. In such a situation there could be no equality of right; security for one side was purchased at the price of the insecurity of the other; "justice" for one at the cost of injustice for the other.

The Allies could have taken another position and have said to Germany:

We do not ask you, the defeated, to accept our domination, but the domination of the law or international rule of conduct by which we ourselves are prepared to abide. We offer you, under it, the same protections we ourselves hope to find. If you accept it, we will undertake to defend it for your security, as we ask you to defend it for ours.

There were, as we know, sporadic efforts to secure the introduction of that principle into the postwar settlement. The Anglo-American-French reciprocal agreement which was to have given France a real security against German aggression (and not one based on the sanctions or guarantees of a Guatemala, or San Domingo, or almost equally remote members of the League); the Treaty of Mutual Assistance, the Geneva Protocol, the Kellogg Pacts, the Locarno Treaties, were all part of these efforts. The theory was that out of such instruments would grow a system in which Germany could find her place with erstwhile victors. But as the very nations which put forward these devices began to repudiate them almost as soon as they were drawn up; and as public opinion in the Allied nations was deeply divided and confused about them, it is not surprising that they did not particularly appeal to the Germans who were able to reply: It is quite clear that you do not yourselves believe in the method to which you ask us to entrust our national destiny.

What *is* the principle about which we were so confused, and concerning which it is so important to be clear if similar bungling in the future is to be avoided?

Where Force Belongs in Society

To clarify the nature of that principle in the simplest way, let us note its operation within a given state—the United States or Great Britain. In those states we have a variety of rival parties or groups—Republican, Democrat, New Deal, anti-New Deal, Labor, Socialist, Communist; and in England, Conservative, Liberal, Labour, and Communist parties, to say nothing of such powerful groups as the

Trade-Unions, Employers Federations, the Co-operative Societies, and similar organizations.

Now, neither in the United States nor in Britain do we attempt to maintain order and law by saying: "All these differences and conflicts of interest must be cleared up if we are to have peace and live in harmony." On the contrary, we keep alive these differences; promote and increase them by new parties, new organizations, continually being formed for the very purpose of challenging some existing interest. We believe that progress and improvement result from the differences, from their free discussion.

But however much the Republican and the Democrat, the New Dealer and anti-New Dealer, the Unionist and the employer, the Tory and the Labour Party may differ, all are agreed on this. If one of those parties or groups attempts to impose its program or settle its difference by armed violence, attempts, that is, to use physical power as the instrument of policy, then all the others, even those sympathetic to the proposed program, support the state or the constitution in resistance to such violence; co-operate in the defense of the victims. If Socialists were murdered, Conservatives would certainly support the efforts of the state to put an end to the killing of Socialists, as rapidly as Socialists would co-operate in the similar defense of Conservatives.

Sometimes the conflict of interest between the rival parties who thus nevertheless co-operate for mutual defense in resistance to violence, is exceedingly deep. In Britain, for instance, the possessors of wealth have seen their holdings steadily encroached upon and eaten away by the very sweeping Social Securities programs of the Labour Party and the Trade-Unions, until, under the impact of war, we see all the great incomes swept entirely away. (No one in the country has a net income of more than $25,000 and only about two hundred persons in the whole of Great Britain have, net, more than $10,000 a year.) There has certainly been no "freezing of the status quo" in the matter of property merely because the constitution possessed preponderant power. Nor have the members of that British oligarchy wearing old school ties, of which we have been hearing a

good deal of late, resisted by armed power the immense encroach-
ments upon their incomes and the liquidation of their properties
through heavy death duties and other means. (Aspects of this problem are dealt with in the next chapter.)

The possessing classes of the American nation have never shown
themselves less ready than the British Conservatives to support
constitutional government in disarming any political party, even
though it be of their own color, that should resort to armed violence.
Even if a Ku Klux Klan proclaimed itself the defender of property
and began murdering Communists as proof of it, we could certainly
count upon the bulk of the Republican Party, as much as upon New
Deal Democrats, to put such Kluxers where they ought to be. We
should *not* find property taking sides with the armed party and
challenging the constitution, initiating thus the class war of the
Marxist forecast. For even "property" would know that it had at
least this common interest with its political rivals, namely the prevention of armed anarchy, the interest not to be killed. Despite
communist assertions to the contrary, civil war is not the only instrument of social change.

The Basic Common Interest

This point—that groups deeply divided in material interest can
nevertheless possess *some* common interest, can combine in the defense of a code or constitution designed in the first instance for common security against violence—has been developed at some length,
because it bears pertinently upon some of the confusions (and
among the chief) which have stood in the way of doing what might
have been done to prevent the onslaught of the totalitarian powers.
Influential sections both Right and Left have taken the ground that
there could be no common interest upon which to base collective
resistance to violence as such. It has been persistently represented
that the interest in law and order professed by the opponents of
Germany was not really an interest in the prevention of violence, but
only an interest in preventing change; that the common interest

in opposing Germany was the interest in the freezing of the status quo to the permanent disadvantage of Have-not states like Germany.

It seems a little difficult to believe at this date that a school of "realists" actually did preach the impossibility of common action against aggression. They not only preached it, but had very great influence. The confusions which they promulgated may, unless dispelled, be as disastrous in the future as they have proved in the past.

Professor H. E. Carr, for some years of the British Foreign Office, and for some years Professor of International Relations in the University of Wales, published just before the outbreak of the present war a book entitled *Twenty Years of Crisis* wherein he enters into an argument with Professor Toynbee who had written in respect of one of the crises provoked by totalitarian aggression, that, after all, "international law and order were in the true interests of the whole of mankind, whereas the desire to perpetuate the reign of violence in international affairs was an anti-social desire which was not even in the ultimate interests of the citizens of the handful of states that officially professed this benighted and anachronistic creed."

Of this view, Professor Carr remarks that it is an argument "compounded of platitude and falsehood in about equal parts," going on to explain that it is "a familiar tactic of the privileged" (Britain being, in this case, the privileged), "to throw moral discredit on the underprivileged" (Germany being the underprivileged), "by depicting them as disturbers of the peace; and this tactic is as readily applied internationally as within the national community." Throughout much of the book this general view that if you are for peace it merely means that you want to keep what you've got, is repeated and emphasized in various forms, thus:

> Just as the ruling class in a community prays for domestic peace which guarantees its own security and predominance and denounces class war which might threaten them, so international peace becomes a special vested interest of predominant Powers.

"There can be no such thing," this writer goes on to explain, "as a common or collective resistance to aggression, nor is it any more

moral to resist aggression than to commit it, for readiness to fight
to prevent change is just as immoral as readiness to fight to enforce
it." (Please note here the confusion between fighting to outlaw
violence and fighting to outlaw change.)

All our high falutin' about fighting for the interests of mankind
are, in Professor Carr's view, so much bunk. We are fighting for our
own interests as against the interests of the disadvantaged states.
There are no "interests of mankind"; there is properly speaking no
general interest. When this talk of the "general interest" is analyzed,
it is "revealed as the transparent disguise of selfish vested interest."
Indeed, Professor Carr comes near to saying that we are just about
as much to blame for the war as the totalitarians. He writes:

> It is a moot point whether the politicians and publicists of the
> satisfied Powers, who have attempted to identify international morality
> with security, law and order and other time-honoured slogans of
> privileged groups, do not bear as large a share of responsibility for
> the disaster as the politicians and publicists of the dissatisfied powers,
> who brutally denied the validity of an international morality so con-
> stituted (p. 289).

It is eloquent of much in Britain's way of managing things that
at the outbreak of the present war, Professor Carr, author of the
passages just quoted, was appointed as Director of the Foreign
Division of the Ministry of Information, whose job it was to explain
and justify Britain's case to the world, particularly, presumably, to
the United States, then neutral.

Why the Peace Failed

Let us see how in fact the Allies failed to use their power after the
last war as the foundation of some nascent code or constitution
designed to eliminate violence as far as possible in international relations.

As soon as the Peace Conference had assembled in Paris and had
addressed itself to redrawing the map of Europe, it faced repeatedly
this kind of situation: Some state—one of the old or one of the new,

with the nomenclature which then seemed somewhat comic and artificial—would present claims to a frontier which, the experts would point out, grossly violated the principle of nationality or self-determination, violated it by the inclusion of populations who certainly did not desire to be included. Whereupon the state concerned would reply:

If we draw the frontier as you desire we shall be weak. The frontier will not be strategic and we shall lack raw materials needed for defense. If we are attacked as the result of acceding to your wishes, will you defend us?

And the Allied Powers in reply would usually mumble indecisively, or say decisively, No.

Whereupon, of course, the state in question would retort:

We keep our immoral frontier. Self-preservation is the first law. Our people would not forgive suicide on behalf of the higher morality.

This sort of situation was illustrated most strikingly and tragically in the case of France herself. Clemenceau and Foch had at the outset of the peace negotiations demanded a buffer independent Rhineland State: a complete Rhine frontier. To all such proposals looking to the break-up of Germany both Wilson and Lloyd George strongly demurred. Yet the French continued to point out that there would soon be twice as many Germans as Frenchmen in the world. Where would France find her security? Finally, as the world knows, a Tripartite Guarantee was drawn up under which Britain and the United States undertook to help in the defense of France if attacked by Germany. That arrangement was never ratified either in London or in Washington. From the moment of the failure of that ratification began the disintegration of the peace. The forces which culminated in the Second World War were then set in motion.

In both America and Britain the same kind of opinion in respect to the war and the future preservation of peace began to manifest itself. In Britain there was great irritation at France, both for her "everlasting demands for guarantees" and for her bad behavior toward Germany, culminating in the Ruhr invasion. In the United States the postwar reaction, disillusion and irritation expressed itself in censure of most of the European victors, particularly Britain. The isolationism which in America expressed itself in the immediate repudiation of the League and the destruction of Wilson, expressed itself in England in the early stages of the postwar developments, by a fairly persistent refusal to furnish any guarantees to France which the French government considered at all adequate.

Behind that refusal lay a curious confusion of thought concerning French behavior to Germany. That behavior was often bad, but motivated mainly by fear of Germany's recovery, when the German eighty million would face the French forty. French policy was largely therefore directed at the prevention of that recovery. Britain saw that there could be neither peace nor prosperity in Europe so long as Germany was artificially prevented from working her way back to normal economic welfare. What Britain failed fully to see was that the way to obtain French assent to German recovery was to offer France complete guarantees of security in return for good French behavior toward the Weimar Republic (which had, in its early years, elements that could have been made the basis of a fruitful co-operation with Europe). France made repeated attempts to secure some kind of substitute for the Anglo-American guarantee offered by Wilson and Lloyd George. There were a number of proposals which suffered the same fate as the Tripartite Guarantee, proposals provisionally accepted by British representatives but which then failed of ratification in London. There was Robert Cecil's Treaty of Mutual Assistance, repudiated by the Labour government which came into office shortly after it had been arranged in Geneva. The Labour government itself then produced the Geneva Protocol, which was in its turn repudiated by the Conservative government which followed, and which in its turn began the framing of the Locarno group of treaties, themselves subject to severe Conservative criticism and which therefore inspired no very lively faith among the French.

Insecurity, not Grievances, the Cause of War

The failures of public opinion of that time stemmed mainly from confusion as to the proper role of power in the maintenance of justice, and so of peace, dealt with a few pages back.

As soon as opinion in Britain had got over its wartime anti-Germanism, and wanted mainly peace with Germany, the British public began to regard any military arrangement with France, any guarantee given her, as a move directed against Germany, as "alliance-building," whose purpose it was to "keep Germany down." The view that the way to secure better treatment of Germany was to give sound military guarantees to France, was a view extremely difficult to put across. Yet it lay at the very core of the situation in those early years. The system of guarantees ran counter to nineteenth-century liberal-pacifist feelings and views of peacemaking. The nineteenth-century laissez-faire view was that the international anarchy would be quite workable if nations exercised good will to one another, and "talked over their differences reasonably." The way to peace was to resolve differences, not to threaten each other with force. The correction of injustices, of bad frontiers, of economic nationalism, was regarded as the *alternative* to collective security, oblivious of the fact that in nine cases out of ten the injustices, the bad frontiers, and the economic nationalisms arose out of the fears of insecurity, the absence of any defense outside a country's own power, strategic position, and self-sufficiency. Justice is not the alternative to mutual security; mutual security is the means by which justice may be made possible; its indispensable condition.

The history of the war itself should have been a warning in that respect. More than one good historian has pointed out that not for years had Anglo-German relations been so free from definable and specific difference as in the first half of the year 1914. Edward Grey indeed made the remark in the early part of that year, "My difficulty in coming to a settlement with Germany is that there is nothing to settle, no grievance, no difference that a man can get hold of." Britain had no grievance against Germany save the supreme grievance that Germany's victory would deprive Britain of all means of defense. Twenty-five years later Britain was once more to declare war against Germany, for the same reason: not because Britain herself had been attacked, not because Germany had done injury to Britain, but because the conquest of others would endanger Britain's security.

The Role of Pseudo-Pacifism

In this period of the twenties the true nature of the problem which faced mankind became badly obscured by the half-truth of certain pacifist-sounding slogans. "The road to peace is to satisfy the just claims of nations, to remedy their just grievances." But the first and last claim of nations, as of every living thing, is some means of self-preservation. If, in order to live, to be able to defend its right to existence, a nation must do injustice, it will do injustice—if indeed there is any form of "justice" which can demand suicide. In such a situation the remedy is to devise a form of defense which will not involve injustice. In case after case we saw nations retaining power over alien populations because not to do so would endanger national security: deprive a nation, nervous about its defense, of some strategic harbor or of some necessary raw material in wartime. The only means of meeting the case would have been for the international community—or *an* international community, a group of nations forming a nucleus international community—to have said to the nations so acting, "In return for your fulfillment of the demands of justice we will undertake to defend you if you are attacked; and we will ask you to help in our defense if we are attacked." But whenever it looked as though some such nascent international community was about to come into being, that a nucleus was being formed, either in Paris or in Geneva, this pseudo-pacifist confusion began to bedevil public opinion. (It was not of course the only opposing factor, but it was a very important one.) "You don't make peace by threatening to go to war" was a favorite slogan in those circles at that time. This slogan overlooked the fact that every nation in the world was trying to maintain peace by threatening to go to war; was, that is, threatening to go to war if anyone attacked it. Those who used such slogans were themselves in favor of Britain maintaining her own armed powers; in favor of threatening to use them, but only if British interests were attacked. The threat, "If you attack our individual interests we will fight," was regarded as an entirely moral, socially minded position, compatible with peace and good morality. For a group of nations to combine for mutual defense and to say "Attack one and you attack all" was regarded as provocative warmongering.

A Bit of Secret History

How disastrously these confusions were affecting the early postwar relations with France, even in very high places in Great Britain, and were giving a disastrous twist to the development of events, was brought home to this writer in the early months of the first Labour government in Britain by an incident, not heretofore related.

It will be recalled that shortly after the formation of that first Labour government, Edouard Herriot had become Premier of France. Herriot came to London to discuss Anglo-French relations with MacDonald. Herriot happened to have been a reader of mine, and we knew each other slightly. On the evening of his arrival in London, and before his meeting with the Prime Minister, he asked me to go to see him at his hotel. There followed a conversation, the essence of which is about as follows:

HERRIOT: I have asked you to come to see me because I happen to know you and your work, and I understand that you have worked with MacDonald in the past and know him well. As I am about to see him, it would be, I think you will agree, in the common interest of our two countries, if I understood his point of view, his outlook, his mind. I want you to help me so to do.

ANGELL: It is true that I have known MacDonald for many years and have worked with him closely in the past. But I am not sure that I know his mind. But go ahead.

HERRIOT: My real purpose of course in coming to see MacDonald is to find out if, at long last, this country will give a permanent, unequivocal guarantee to support France in the event of German attack. I won't labor the point of how much that would do for the stabilization of Europe, and the future peace of the world—to say nothing of the improvement of the relations with Germany. All that is familiar ground to you. What will MacDonald reply when I ask him if his government is prepared to give that guarantee for which we have been asking so long, and so persistently?

ANGELL: As I warned you, I cannot be positive as to his reaction to that question. But perhaps it would help you if I were to tell you how one member at least of MacDonald's party—and one close to him—this one, would reply if he had MacDonald's responsibility.

HERRIOT: By all means. Go ahead.

ANGELL: I would reply that we cannot possibly give you an unconditional guarantee, a blank check. You know what has been the course of French policy of late and the tendency of certain forces within France. To give you a blanket guarantee would, at this moment, put a premium upon perhaps the worst elements of French policy—elements which are among those you yourself fight. If an unconditional guarantee were to have the effect of strengthening the more violent anti-German elements, French policy might become so provocative that the Germans would fight with bare fists; and we would find ourselves in a war that better behavior could have avoided.

HERRIOT: Of course I see your point; and of course I have provided for it. You want some guarantee of good political behavior on our part so that you will not be involved in the results of bad policy which is not yours. I am ready to make some such provision as this: We will not call upon you to aid us in defense against Germany unless and until any dispute which you feel ought to be arbitrated has been submitted to arbitration and Germany has refused: or some arrangement along those general lines. This should give "the guarantee of good political behavior" for which you ask.

ANGELL: This is indeed an advance.[3] But I feel that a still further condition is necessary, namely, that we should be free to make precisely the same arrangement with Germany.

HERRIOT: Well, I have faced that too, and am ready to agree.

ANGELL: Forgive the question, but have you talked over this aspect of the matter with your military people? The soldiers are likely to find terrific objections to an arrangement of that kind.

HERRIOT: I had Nollet, my minister of war, travel in the train with me from Paris to Calais in order that we could talk over that precise detail. He has annotated a memorandum which I had prepared. (Herriot hunts in his dispatch case.) Here on this page you will see two questions which cover the point of your query; and you see his reply.

ANGELL: (having glanced at the typewritten memo and having noted a penciled "*oui*, N.") : This is really tremendous. If you can pull it off with MacDonald your visit should be a turning point in Europe's history.

HERRIOT: Now, I have a favor to ask of you and I think I'm wise in asking it. Go and see MacDonald now, tomorrow; go over the arguments of this case. As an old personal friend you can do it.

ANGELL: MacDonald is not an easy man to advise, and he does not easily take counsel with his friends. But even if it does not make it easier for you I don't think it should make it more difficult.

HERRIOT: I want you to go, if you will.

Herriot added certain cautions about discretion, the reasons for which have long since disappeared. Thus this story of that talk.

I saw MacDonald; reminded him of the way the French still fumed and fretted, and that of course Herriot would once more put the old question: What will England do if the Boche once more attacks? "And I shall tell him," said MacDonald after some talk, "that if France behaves well there is virtually no chance that the Boche will attack."

---

[3] The reader will note that this conversation took place a year or two before the Locarno group of treaties were drawn up.

I tried to put to MacDonald the difficulties of Herriot's position if he should return empty-handed to a critical chamber, asked him if he proposed that Herriot should report to his chamber in some such terms as these: "I have seen Mr. MacDonald with reference to guarantees, and he has assured me that if only we behave nicely to the Germans there is no danger that they will attack us."

Well, in any case, MacDonald argued, Britain was going to give no more guarantees. I remember him saying something to this effect: "The end of all these undertakings to go to war if this, that, or the other thing happens, is that we *shall* go to war. I see that as the likely outcome of Bob Cecil's Treaty of Mutual Assistance, and I'm against it. I imagine from your talk that you are rather taken with it. I think you're getting into bad company."

And so Herriot went back to Paris, empty-handed.

Confusions about Commitments

This phrase of MacDonald's about "all these commitments leading us back to war" expressed one of the three or four outstanding confusions of that time. The assumption underlying it is that commitments lead to war; whereas the outstanding lesson of the First World War is that nation after nation was dragged into it precisely because it had *not* been committed beforehand. When Lloyd George was asked once whether World War No. 1 could have been avoided, he—the man who was prime minister during the greater part of the war, whose contacts with the heads of governments involved were as intimate as those of any man living—made this reply: "Yes. The Great War could have been prevented. If those nations which did in fact enter the field against Germany had said beforehand that they would do so unless Germany changed her policy, there would have been no war; for Germany would have changed her policy."

It comes to this: If those nations which were involved in the war had said beforehand that they would do in given circumstances precisely what they did in those circumstances—they would not have had to do it.

There is nothing obscure or complicated in such an assertion. It is a mere statement of the principle of preventive power, upon which social order rests. Germany simply did not believe that the policy she followed in 1914 would bring countries like America into the field against her. If she *had* believed it she would not have followed the policy she did. Power can have no preventive—peacekeeping—effect unless it is realized by those who would break the peace that it will be used against them. This involves commitments.

Another confusion of that time resulted from the loose use of the word "war." It sufficed for a politician to ask of any proposed warning or sanction, whether directed at Germany in Spain or the Rhineland, or Italy in Abyssinia, or Japan in China, "Do you want war?" for the advocate of resistance commonly to be silenced. It was of course a dishonest question. Nobody wanted war; but the country did want defense, and whether the people realized it or not, they would fight when the defense of the country clearly demanded it. What they did not see was that if force was to be used as a deterrent of certain hostile acts, those likely to commit those acts must be quite clear that the force *would* be used if they did commit them.

Statesmen of that period were always using such phrases as "the greatest interest of our country is peace." It was a muddleheaded if not insincere statement. For if some foreign nation began invasion of the country, even the statesmen in question would call for war, a war of defense; which would mean that he was putting defense before peace, thus proclaiming that he did not believe peace, but defense to be "the greatest interest of his country." Some of us urged —vainly—at that time that inevitably there would come a point when the country would not stand the continued advance of the totalitarians any further, and would call a halt. If that halt were called early it would mean peace; if it were called late it would mean war. Yet all counsels for *early* warning were regarded by the public as "warmongering." "If these people," said one critic writing just after

Chamberlain's return from Munich with "peace in our time," "had had their way, we would have been involved in at least three wars—one over Manchuria, one over the Rhineland, and one over Abyssinia." A favorite slogan of the Abyssinian period was that "sanctions mean war." The truth being of course that if the sanctions had been certain, if Britain, even acting alone, had made it plain to Mussolini in 1934 that she would defend Ethiopia precisely as she would defend Kenya or the Cape, the Duce would no more have dreamed of attacking Ethiopia than he did of attacking the Cape. There would have been no war if sanctions, including the ultimate military sanction, had been certain. War came because the sanctions were uncertain, doubtful, and from Mussolini's point of view, therefore, worth risking.

In the First World War the Germans had no clear notion of what they were running into. The nations which were to suffer from their attack had managed to leave Germany completely in the dark, as to what would result from the German action, as Mr. Lloyd George makes clear in his memoirs. He declares that the Kaiser had not the remotest idea that the line he was taking would be regarded by other European states as an attack upon them of a kind that would provoke their armed resistance. Mr. Lloyd George's words are these:

> I am convinced after a careful perusal of all the documents available on all sides that the Kaiser never had the remotest idea that he was plunging—or being plunged—into a European war . . . He was not anticipating a costly war but a cheap diplomatic triumph. . . . Had it been made clear in time to the Kaiser that Britain would make war upon Germany, if she invaded Belgium, he and his advisers would have paused to confer ere it became too late to withdraw. He had not accumulated sufficient stores of food or raw materials to face the blockade of the British Fleet. A halt of a few weeks to confer would have taken the nations near to the winter months when the march of gigantic armies would have been impeded in the West and impossible in the East. Mobilization had begun in Austria, Russia, France, and Germany, and war had actually been declared between these Powers

before Britain delivered her ultimatum about Belgium. It was then too late to recall the legions who were already hurrying to battle.[4]

So it would seem that not merely did the potential aggressor not know what others would regard as an attack; these others did not themselves know.

"No sovereign or leading statesman in any of the belligerent countries sought or desired war—certainly not a European war," insists Mr. Lloyd George. The Austrian foreign minister wanted a punitive expedition against Serbia. Had he realized that it would involve war with Russia, Italy, and Rumania, supported by Britain, France, and ultimately America, he would have modified the terms of the ultimatum or accepted Serbia's answer, which was abject enough to satisfy even Austrian pride. But he was convinced that Russia would not face war with Germany. The Czar had retreated over the much more important question of the annexation of Bosnia without striking a blow. His army now was not much better prepared than it had been then. On the other hand, Germany had considerably strengthened hers. So the moment the Kaiser gave his word that he would back up Austria's demands, Berchtold had no doubt that Russia would give in and, if Serbia were still obdurate, war with her would be a small matter. What about Germany?

France shrank from war, and there was nothing further from the mind of Britain or her Government at the end of July, 1914, than the staging of a Continental war. The negotiations were botched by everybody engaged in directing them. It is incredible that so momentous an issue should have been handled in so unbusinesslike and casual a manner. When a collision seemed inevitable engine drivers and signalmen lost their heads and pulled the wrong levers. The stokers alone did their work. In politics one is accustomed to haphazard methods which produce minor disasters that overturn ministries. But this was a question of life and death for Empires, Kingdoms, and Republics— and for millions of their subjects.[5]

---

[4] *War Memoirs of David Lloyd George*, Ivor Nicholson and Watson, London, Volume VI, Page 3346.

[5] *Ibid.*

In saying that no force, however great, can possibly deter aggression unless the potential aggressor knows that he will have to meet it, knows, that is, what the defender will regard as attack, one is once more in the region of the self-evident, of truisms. But they are, also once more, truisms which are daily, all but universally ignored.

The Best the Enemy of the Better

During all the period between the Japanese aggression of 1931 and the German occupation of Prague, which marked the end of the appeasement policy, there was a tragic tendency for opponents of collective defense to make the best the enemy of the better, the ideal the enemy of the possible. And as the lesson on that point may have relevance to the problems which face us now it is worth considering.

The opponents of sanctions against Japan began, very inappropriately in the circumstances, to discover the superiority of the federal method over the League method of ensuring peace. They disinterred the arguments of the federalists about the difficulty and danger of coercing a state. These arguments were doubtless, *in abstracto*, entirely sound. A federation of states is doubtless much superior as a form of international society to a mere League, or Concert of Powers, or Grand Alliance or Coalition, or what you will. But that debate was quite irrelevant to the situation which then confronted Western Europe, and was later to confront this country. The problem which then faced us—and faces us all now in still more acute form—was and is the problem of resistance to an advancing aggression. That resistance could only then be achieved by common action between separate nations. It can only be achieved now by common action between separate nations. The particular constitutional form of that association was not the vital thing. The vital thing was to get common resistance to growing aggression. To say, as so many did say at that time: "We cannot take action together against Japan or Italy or Germany because Jefferson and other federalists have proved that you cannot successfully coerce a state or a nation; that this notion of collective action against nations is on the wrong principle and that what we ought to have is not a League but a federation"—such an attitude, quite common at that time, often taken by men of considerable political experience (one such became a British ambassador to the United States), seemed to this writer at least about the last word in unrealism; though it was the line taken by many who insisted that above all they were realists.

The League at that time existed; it had acquired certain loyalties; and however clumsy the instrument it would have been better to use it for the necessary operation rather than have the patient die for lack of the operation. Assume, as the critics kept telling us, that a coalition of sovereign states was the wrong method. It is, however, precisely that method which we are now compelled to use in organizing the common action of the thirty United Nations. The United Nations are even further from the federative principle than the League would have been.

When the United States, early in the nineteenth century, made herself the protector of every republic upon this hemisphere, the job must have seemed of appalling dimensions. And her unilateral action was, in some sense without doubt, offensive to those she was protecting. But, with the help of the British Navy, it worked; and later the unilateral policy was transformed into a multilateral and reciprocal one.

Some similar development from unilateral to multilateral policy would have resulted if Britain had, about 1934, proclaimed her Monroe Doctrine in respect to Article XVI of the Covenant, and declared that for her part she would fulfill its obligations, alone if necessary; that she reserved the right to regard an attack upon any state protected by the Covenant as an attack upon Britain. The proclamation would of course have been directed particularly at Mussolini and would have made it plain that in the matter of sanctions in the Ethiopian affair Britain meant business; that Ethiopia would be aided in her defense (actually Simon put an embargo upon munitions to Abyssinia), the Suez Canal closed to Italian arms, and much more to the same effect. Britain by such action would probably have dragged much of the League after her; and the unilateral action might well have become multilateral and collective.

It is collective action by thirty nations, of the nonfederal kind, upon which the defense of civilization now rests. It will be wise to transform the present machinery into some institution of a more federal type. But if the type of non-federal collective action we now take had been taken earlier, we might have avoided war; and the development toward federation would still have been possible.

Coercion or Defense?

The long arguments of those days about the impossibility of coercing governments were obviously, then, beside the point. We were seriously told that we could not go to China's aid because that would amount to the "coercion of Japan"! One would have thought that it was more properly defined as the prevention of coercion of China by Japan. If I am attacked by a man with an ax and I take the ax from him do I thus "coerce" him? If he is attacking a neighbor with an ax and I take the ax from him, is that "coercion"?

One would have said of that time that the general conception of the function of force in civilization was marked by complete confusion. Such phrases as "force is no remedy," "right, not might," "reason, not violence," were flung about easily and casually but only served to confuse things. If a nation says to a threatening neighbor: "I want our quarrel settled by third-party judgment, impartial reason looking into all the facts," and the neighbor replies: "I intend to settle it by imposing my judgment on you because I believe that I am right and you are weaker," then as the result of the former's resistance to the latter both may go to war, both may use "force." But they will be doing so for completely opposed purposes. The first will be using force in order that third-party judgment, reason, may come into play; the second in order that those things may not. The first will be using force to make reason, discussion, possible; the second will be using force to make those things impossible. What, as applied to that situation, is the meaning of such phrases as "Force v. Reason" or "Force v. Law"? Without the force of resistance to aggression the dispute could never reach the area of reason or law.

This simple distinction was often confused by the introduction into the question of stopping aggression the irrelevant question of the merits of the dispute. We could not, it was argued, "interfere" in the Sino-Japanese dispute because we could not judge its merits. Japan might have just causes of grievance. Yet all we needed to know was what we did know: that China was willing to defer the dispute to third-party judgment and Japan was not; that Japan insisted upon being her own judge and making war. We should, of course, have taken the line (as already indicated elsewhere in these pages) to Japan: You may be entirely right in the dispute and China wrong; in that case we will help you bring the fact to light and use our influence with China for redress. But you shall not make war upon China in order to be your own judge, imposing your own judgment by violence.

Our first task is to end the international anarchy; to put our collective power behind law, the law against violence and aggression.

But there are many learned folk—and reformers at that—who do not believe this to be the first task at all. And as their indifference or opposition to the task may be serious, their view must be considered.

The war has come because of the extreme political conservatism inherent in nationalism and isolationism; owing to the refusal to surrender sufficient of national sovereignty to make possible an international society. Yet many social reformers insist that the necessary political revolution is secondary and will come of itself if the present economic constitution of Western nations is sufficiently transformed, or is abolished. This puts the cart before the horse. Social transformations were taking place before the war, but because they did not bring with them the necessary political changes they are now threatened by triumphant Nazidom. To protect the social advance at home we must produce the political revolution in international relations, for which unity is indispensable. This may be imperiled by promoting a domestic revolution at home at the moment we are fighting a desperate foreign war. A note on the economic and social transformations in Britain.

CHAPTER V

Which Revolution Matters Most?

THE last ten years in the United States and the last twenty in Britain have seen a very sharp acceleration of social reform, of the process of "socialization." The New Deal in this country had already, by the eve of the present war, gone far enough to excite in some conservative circles intense hostility to the administration and to President Roosevelt, a hostility, however, which, on the whole, the New Deal forces were successfully meeting. In Britain we had seen the steady growth of a system of social security more far-reaching and elaborate than that which any other modern state (except possibly New Zealand) could show. Unemployment and health insurance, workmen's compensation, Factory Acts, Old Age Pensions, Widows' Pensions, had not merely been established; every year saw legislative additions to them in one way or another. Organized Labor has so far asserted its power as to have been able, not merely to build up the most powerful and unified Trade-Union System in history, but twice within twenty years, to have taken over the government, acting through its political instrument, the British Labour Party. An income tax which is, and has been for a long time, the highest in the world was beginning—through expenditure of its product upon the social services—to redistribute the national income with increasing regard to the needs of the people as a whole. Today of course there are no more great incomes in Britain, and the stiffest death duties in the world have hastened this process of redistribution. The great consumer's co-operatives, run almost entirely by manual workers, have so developed that they have become one of the biggest big businesses of the country. More and more have capital and finance been brought under national control by a body of banking, insurance, commercial, and industrial legislation which is every

year increased, and every increase of which tightens the control of
the community. New forms of control like those which operate in
the case of the Port of London Authority, the amalgamations of the
London Transport System, the British Broadcasting Corporation,
have broken new ground in the way of combining public control and
private enterprise; virtual public ownership with the minimum of
bureaucratic machinery. Meanwhile, the workers have managed to
secure the establishment of Management-Labour Boards in every
factory, so that today the worker has a recognized part, through
definitely organized representation, in the management of the concern in which he is employed.

Obviously this process is not now going to come to a full stop. It is
indicative of a deep-seated tendency, a tendency which will continue.
Even before the present war, when socialization had not been carried to the extent to which it has been carried since, an eminent
British Labour leader said to the present writer that more practical
and productive Socialism had been put into operation in Britain
during the preceding twenty years than in Russia. In Russia, indeed,
the tendency had been in the opposite direction—away from "pure"
Socialism to the acceptance of features which would have horrified
the Socialist doctrinaires of the 1917 revolution, as characteristic of
the capitalist and bourgeois society it was their intention to overthrow.

Be that as it may, we cannot with any truth describe the social
and economic condition of the United States or Britain as static,
frozen, only to be broken by revolution and violence. It is mislead-
ing to talk of the "prewar status quo" in Britain. There was no status
quo, since it was changing all the time. The changes were great and
made peacefully—peace being indeed necessary to their effective
working, since the actual operation of Socialism depends upon administrative competence, an atmosphere of co-operation, not of
civil war, hatred, and violence.[1]

---

[1] Mr. Justice Felix Frankfurter of the United States Supreme Court, in an
address before the City College of New York (Sept. 30, 1942), said:

It is a significant fact that economic inequalities are strikingly less in Britain
than they are in this country. That in all of Britain last year there were only

But if on the social side in Britain we have had relatively rapid and sweeping change, on the side of international politics in the political structure of Europe as a whole, we find extreme conservatism, a stone wall opposition to even the most timid innovations. While the institutions of private property, capitalism, banking, commerce have been undergoing profound modification, the relations of nations, based on the complete sovereignty and independence of each, have remained organically unaltered ever since the rise of the nation-state. The League of Nations was not, after all, a very revolutionary proposal so far as its first proposals were concerned. Its innovations were so hedged about with saving clauses that the most nervous might (one would suppose) have been reassured. But the Tories, who have not been able notably to stem the steady—even if too slow—advance of social reform, have been able (as in the case of the anti-Wilson, anti-League, anti-Court campaigns) to block completely any organic change whatever in the international field.

Yet it is conservatism in this field which threatens to bring the radicalism in the other to naught, to frustrate all advances made in the social field: as the most advanced of the Socialists and the Communists now avow. A Nazi victory would mean the end of any kind of Socialism under which free men would care to live.

In the presence of this phenomenon of steady if not very dramatic advance on the social side, and utter stagnation on the political, the attitude of the more advanced forces of the Left, the Socialists and Communists, has usually been a strange one. They have for the most part taken the line that political changes, like those inherent in the League proposal, were of entirely secondary importance; sometimes they have energetically opposed the League (this was the case particularly before Russia's entrance into it) on the ground that it

---

eighty persons to whom the tax-gatherers left an income of five thousand pounds, is a fact of revolutionary implications—far-reaching changes peacefully accomplished but nonetheless revolutionary in their social consequences. They are consequences that make of our traditional old school-tie, Tory ridden, class-bound, anti-democratic picture of England an obsolete caricature, but too often a mischief-making caricature still. It is an untrue picture of England, not unexploited by the enemies of this country, that for too long has confused too many minds in this country as to the nature of this conflict.

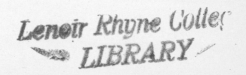

tended to crystallize or freeze the economic status quo, and because it was composed of capitalist governments. When there was not direct opposition, there was often apathy based on the theory that, if only fundamental economic change could be brought about, the international problem with its complex of nationalism, isolationism, competition for national power, would solve itself. War, we were told with infinite repetition, was the result of capitalism and would disappear when capitalism was abolished; the line-up of force in the world would, we were also told, have little relation to nationalism; the clash would be that of competing capitalist states, or between those states and Russia and the forces of social advance for which she stood. The events are sufficient commentary on these propositions.

The point, however, which concerns us now is this: If the present war is a revolutionary war only to be won by revolutionary methods, then the revolution must be primarily, at its base, political. *For if the political revolution in the international field does not take place the economic one becomes impossible or worthless.*

Once more one must appeal to the basic fact of this war. The Nazi power has overcome a score of states and made all their social gains meaningless, not because they were "capitalist" but because they were nationalist, isolationist, because they would not combine, co-operate for defense. The French bourgeoisie may have hated Russia; but it also refused effective co-operation with Britain, effective support of the League. If the dominant motive of the European capitalist governments was fear or hatred of Russia, then, presumably they would have combined against Russia; and would have accepted the German proposals made so repeatedly for an anti-Russian pact. Yet the offer of Hitler to Britain "Let Germany expand eastward and we will leave the west alone" was refused, even by Chamberlain. When made again through Hess just previous to the German attack on Russia, and when England was in a position of deadly peril, it was refused by the Conservative-Capitalist Churchill; and when Germany did strike at Russia, Churchill did not hesitate one second to ally himself definitely, completely, with the Communist-Soviet power. Hitler's offer to Western "capitalist" states to facilitate his war against Russia was refused; his offer to Russia in 1939 to facilitate his war against the West was accepted.

There would of course have been no Russo-German agreement if in the years before 1939 there had been a *political* revolution in the relationship of European states; if notions of national sovereignty and independence had been modified as much as the institution of private property had been modified in the preceding thirty or forty years.

The most revolutionary step taken in the political, international field, in modern times, was taken by a Tory-Capitalist prime minister when he offered an Act of Union to France, an act which would have made the two countries one. Yet there is a section of the British Left which has campaigned against Mr. Churchill on the ground that he is not sufficiently revolutionary in a social sense. They attach, it would seem, very little importance to the political revolution by which alone the social revolution now going on can be protected. Some of the social revolutionaries would indeed slow up the revolution in the political field.

Thus, Professor Laski, who is continually demanding initiation of a profound social revolution during the war, is opposed to the kind of Union which Mr. Churchill offered France being effected between the United States and Great Britain, because, one gathers, the United States has not yet made sufficient advance toward the socialization of property. Professor Laski accuses Mr. Churchill of refusing to "blast the foundation of the old society," and of fighting now to prevent such blasting. But in the political field Mr. Churchill is ready for "blasting" where Professor Laski is hesitant and wants to wait.

At the 1941 Labour Party Conference, Professor Laski, in support of one of the resolutions, spoke in these terms:

> This is a revolutionary war of the twentieth century, and, blasting the foundations of the old society, it is imposing new fundamental principles and setting new problems which, at our peril, we have to solve now. . . .

Churchill has agreed this is a people's war. We mean to win it, but we want from him a pledge that from the people's war will issue a people's peace.

So far Churchill has evaded this assurance. So far he has talked of victory in terms of the old world that is dying, not of the new world that is struggling to be born.

The prime minister must stand by the people of Britain not only in their war against vested interests abroad, but also in their war against vested interests at home.

Professor Laski added that "it is time the Labour party made it unmistakably clear that it is not merely a Democratic party, but a Socialist party also."

Emanuel Shinwell, Member of Parliament, declared that the war must be won not only for the purpose of defeating Adolf Hitler and his accomplices, but also to see that capitalism is no longer securely entrenched.[2]

Mr. Laski has recently written that the reverses in Libya are due to the fact that "Mr. Churchill is fighting to preserve the system now in being." He insists that "liberal democracy has broken down" and that the only way that England and America can win the war is to introduce a Socialist or Communist form of economic constitution. He adds:

The roots of the Churchill system are in a soil that is already and obviously exhausted . . . The reverse in Libya is an epitaph upon a system. It is the natural and logical outcome of the effort to wage a revolutionary war without revolutionary means. It is the necessary consequence of a government which seeks to revitalise a society that is dying instead of being urged to hasten the birth of the society that is seeking to be born.[3]

---

[2] Note, however, that the chairman of the conference, who did not belong to the intellectuals but to the trade-union side of the movement, spoke as follows: "We assure Churchill we stand behind him. If he calls us to further sacrifice with the end of winning the war, we will follow. Never has a prime minister had a more loyal party to follow him in this effort than has Churchill in the Labour Party."

[3] *The New Statesman and Nation*, July 11, 1942.

To question the wisdom of opening this second social and political front at home in war time is not of course to question the validity or desirability of Socialism as such, or of any particular form of Socialism. If our first purpose is the maintenance of a national unity indispensable to victory, we are not concerned with the ultimate intrinsic merits of Socialism or Capitalism as rival economic systems, but with the form of either which will achieve the largest degree of national consent during war time. As a matter of fact the present war-time economy of Britain is about as Socialist as it could possibly be in the sense of national control of the economic processes; of the activities of all the people, and in the sense of equality of sacrifice. The dispute is really whether now, in the midst of war, the nation should decide upon the precise economic theory which should govern its life in peacetime. The bourgeois resistance to Socialism (the precise meaning of which has always been a matter of bitter dispute among Socialists) may be very stupid; but it is also quite obviously sincere, and the bourgeois doubts as to the suitability of "Socialism" for peace time conditions are shared by great sections, perhaps indeed the majority, of the nation. For one section to say: "We won't play unless you accept our doctrines for peace, even though you don't believe in them" (which of course is what one form of Socialist, the Communist, did say until Russia was attacked) is not the road to national unity.

Surely the position taken by General de Gaulle is very much sounder. Not only is he not a Socialist, but he stands very much to the Right in French politics. Nevertheless, he welcomes warmly into his ranks Frenchmen of all political opinions—Socialists, Communists, Rightists, Leftists. Indeed there could hardly be a Free French movement at all except on that basis.

As to the two charges so repeatedly made by those of Mr. Laski's school of thought, that British reverses are due to the Capitalist form of British society and that pre-war appeasement is due to the same cause, two questions would seem to arise.

If "Capitalism" explains the British reverses, what explains the German victories?

This commentary prompts the question whether or not the undeniable military efficiency of the Germans, and to a lesser degree that of the Japanese, is due to their Socialism. The most competent armies in this war have been German. They have displayed an efficiency, an ingenuity, an adaptability to new conditions, unequaled by the army of any other people. It serves no good purpose to deny that fact, and it is a grave disservice to the Allied cause to ignore or disguise it. Is the undoubted military efficiency of those armies due to the excellence of their national society? British defeats, we are told, are due to the lack of Socialism. Then what are German and Japanese victories due to?

And so, too, with the argument that the prewar appeasement employed by the British government was due to the class structure in Britain, the desire of the privileged to defend their privileges.

If that is true how do we explain the fact that the supreme act of appeasement, the act which indeed precipitated the war, was committed by Russia?

The present writer would be the very last to recall that bit of history (he is all in favor of forgetting yesterday where by so doing we serve the purposes of today and tomorrow), but for the fact that forgetfulness of it now is exposing us to the danger of bringing about once more that self-same suspicion and disunity which led to the Russian error. Before we support a campaign with the set purpose of undermining confidence in the present political leadership of the democracies, we need to examine the grounds upon which the criticism is based, with the utmost care and skepticism.

The essence of appeasement is this: The prospective aggressor says to those who might defend his prospective victim: "If you will undertake not to interfere with me when I attack this third party, I will undertake to leave you alone; and even give you a share of the booty."

Hitler, as indicated above, repeatedly attempted by that method to secure the neutrality of Britain in his contemplated thrust to the East. It was the standing accusation made by the Communists before the war that the capitalist governments of the West were making just such a deal with Hitler, in respect to Russia. But the bargain which Britain and France refused to entertain (as proved by the fact that they went to war when Hitler did attack Poland) was precisely the kind of bargain which Russia accepted in the Russo-German Nonaggression Pact: Russia undertook to remain neutral while Hitler launched his attacks against Poland and the Western democracies, and received as payment Germany's acquiescence in Russia's annexation of half of Poland, the whole of Lithuania, Latvia, Estonia, and Bessarabia; and in the Russian attack upon Finland.

It was this supreme appeasement of Hitler by Russia which made German aggression possible. Once more the fact is recalled, not for the purpose of recrimination, but in order to remind the reader that the adoption of Socialism by a nation is no guarantee that it will not be compelled to play the old game of power politics in its crudest and most cynical form owing to the absence of that *political* revolution in the international field necessary for the creation of an international society. If the policy actually adopted by Russia had been followed by the "capitalist" governments of the West, the fact would have been accepted as proof positive of the causal connection between capitalism and aggression, as indicating the desperate straits to which the present economic system had been reduced.

But it is not merely the action of a Russian government we have to recall. The extreme Left in Britain, as represented by the British Communist Party and the members of the Independent Labour Party, was opposed to declaration of war upon Germany. For them, as for the Communists in the United States, the war was, during the first twenty months of its course, just another war of rival imperialisms; its prosecution to be opposed. One is obliged, therefore, to ask what would have been the effect upon the fate of democratic civilization if the social revolution Mr. Laski demands had taken place, and if, instead of the gradualist Socialism of the British Labour Party, we had had Marxist Socialism of the kind which brought some seventy

Communists into the French Chamber of Deputies; and if British Socialists had then adopted in respect to Hitler's aggression the same attitude as that taken by Russian Socialists.

In considering the contingency of a more "Left" government in Britain we have to remember that the bitterest opponents of Communism in Britain were not the Conservatives, but the Trade-Unionists; and that in Britain, as elsewhere, the hostility between the various Socialist groups, the differing schools of Socialism, was so deep as to make an agreed Socialist doctrine impossible.

Insistence upon the acceptance of a certain social doctrine by the government of a country, when that country as a whole is not yet converted to the doctrine, is not likely to give us the unity which alone can bring victory—or establish Socialism. One of the services which Britain has done to the cause of the United Nations is to show, at the hour of the greatest need, an ability to put the common cause above doctrinal and all internal minor differences; to show that the Churchills and Bevins, Tories and Socialists, employers and Trade-Unionists can work together. This capacity for compromise, the tolerance of the radical for the weaknesses of the conservative, may have been overdone. But it is that particular quality which, as much as anything else, made possible a resistance that saved the freedom of the world.

It is necessary to recall that fact when we consider Professor Laski's demand that the government go Socialist. And in considering it, we would do well to note, once more, that this war has arisen, not because the states now overrun by Hitler refused to go Socialist, but because they failed to combine or co-operate politically for the purposes of common defense.

Power and the Social Question

When Socialists of the school of Mr. Laski adopt the language of Marx and the class war, implying that the problem of social advance is a problem of transferring power from a privileged class to the people, it is well to note what changes have occurred since the days of Marx; how very much less it is a question of getting power for "the people," and how very much more a question of knowing how to use it for ends of welfare; how very much more a question of avoiding doctrinal conflicts within the ranks of Socialists themselves—conflicts which, it would seem, became so bitter that they can only be resolved by totalitarian methods like those which the Russian government has been obliged to adopt, and which mean the end of such democratic freedoms, as a free press and an opposition free to criticize the government.

Before the industrial revolution—in the eighteenth century, say—a group of peasants obliged to surrender most of the fruits of their labor to their landlord could solve their problem by simple force, if they had it; by assaulting his château, hanging him to his own gatepost; and dividing his land among themselves.

That is hardly the position of workers on, say, a modern railway; they cannot take the property and divide it among themselves—to one a Pullman car, to another a mile of steel rails. Not only is an intricate technology involved, but the railway itself has to be integrated in complicated fashion with the industry, commerce, and finance of the whole country. Otherwise the wages are not forthcoming at the end of the week. The profound difference as to the effectiveness of power, force, between the two situations need not be elaborated. You may have "power" over your automobile if you have a crowbar that can smash it to pieces. Much good may the power do you in the absence of the knowledge of the mechanism.

The change is not confined to economics and technology. This development, illustrated by the coming of railroads, has altered profoundly the psychology of the class war. Industrialized societies tend to become bourgeois rather than "proletarian"; the proportion of white-collar workers tends greatly to increase; the miner's daughter becomes a stenographer, a private secretary, taking on the attitudes and outlook of the bourgeois. The plumber's son goes to college, and so forth.

Perhaps the commonest Marxist interpretation of social development is that just as the end of the eighteenth century brought the middle class into power, and ended the power of the aristocracy, so now the twentieth century is destined to see the end of the power of the middle classes and to bring the workers on top. But this symmetrical neatness does not fit the facts. It would be much truer to say that what is happening now, at least in the United States and Britain, is that the whole society is becoming what we should in the recent past have called middle class. The very wealthy are losing their large incomes through taxation and by other means; the workers are rising to a standard of living which was yesterday that of the middle classes. Moreover, the middle classes themselves have become increasingly "proletarian" in the sense that they have become increasingly a class of technicians and professional folk dependent upon their earnings, not upon industrial commercial exploitation. Temperamentally they may not belong to "labor" and its organizations. Economically their position is similar (particularly in its insecurity); and as there is diminishing difference in their standard of life the "class struggle" has been by-passed through the simple process of merging. Every observant visitor to England these days (notably most of the American correspondents there) testifies to the equalizing tendencies of life in Britain. "Everybody," wrote an American correspondent recently, "is beginning to live at about the same standard. In the subsidized 'British restaurants,' run by the public authorities, you get a better meal usually than at the luxury hotels; everybody seems to dress the same, eat the same, and share the same comforts or discomforts."

It is this "bourgeois" people who have become the "common" people. This does not mean that there are not groups of opposing interests. There have been plenty of opposing interests as between various capitalist groups; as there has at times been bitter rivalry between labor unions. But the peoples of the democracies of western Europe have power now over property, and over their own policy and destiny, if they knew how to use that power and were agreed upon the ends toward which it should be used. Their failures arise not from lack of power but from lack of agreement, both as to method and to ends. The only means by which they can get either the knowledge or the agreement is by certain moral disciplines, which are disagreeable, irksome, at times extremely burdensome. These moral disciplines they will not assume so long as they can be persuaded that the fault for tragedies like the present does not lie in any shortcomings of their own, of "the general public" that is, which must be corrected, but in the wickedness of others, scapegoats upon whom all guilt can be thrown.

The War, Socialism, and the New Order

This present writer happens to be a Socialist in the British Labour Party or the American New Deal sense of the term; to believe that Socialism or socialization in the sense of the increasing control of the community over the economic processes by which it lives is wise, inevitable. But that belief is entirely compatible with the conviction that the problem of so organizing the world as to render impossible attacks upon civilization by a small minority of ruthless gangsters like the Nazis, is primarily a problem of political organization, just as the protection of citizens from murder and robbery is primarily a problem of political organization, resulting finally in police and courts, although much of the murder and the robbery may have economic causes. But we cannot even tackle the economic causes if we do not get an efficiently working political apparatus. You cannot work socialism in a condition of political anarchy. When the capitalist and bourgeois society of the thirteen colonies carried through their political plans which resulted in the Union of the States, and which, with one interruption in the course of more than a century and a half, enabled the States to maintain peace between themselves, and to build up bit by bit a powerful federal government—when they achieved that *political* result, they did not make Socialism more remote; they made the New Deal and whatever form of socialization is to follow it, far more feasible than it would have been if no political union had been formed.

That such a combination for mutual defense—even a very tight and far-reaching combination—is possible without Socialism, this particular detail of American history completely proves. The thirteen English colonies did unite. The Spanish colonies often failed in their efforts toward federal unity, although, like the English colonies, they had a common cultural and historical background. But if the English succeeded where the Spanish failed, it was certainly not due to the fact that Massachusetts or Virginia were less "capitalist" than, say, the Spanish province which afterward became Guatemala or San Salvador. One can go further. If in each American state there had been powerful Socialist parties, a sharp and bitter class cleavage (there was, of course, some such cleavage) and the "Levelers" (as the Socialists of the time were called) in each state had insisted that their particular state go Socialist before it enter the federation, then almost certainly the federation would have failed, and there would have developed north of the Mexican border somewhat the condition which has developed south of it—a number of small independent sovereign states, each with its separate army, tariff, currency, and revolutions. It is extremely doubtful whether these would have survived the assaults of the Holy Alliance; whether the Monroe Doctrine would have been possible, whether these would have been New Deals at all, whether the standard of life in what is now the United States would have been possible.

The view that the thirty United Nations must all become Socialist in order to achieve unity and military competence; or that it will add to such unity or competence for the Socialist minority to compel a Churchill, head of a Conservative party, to accept an economic doctrine in which neither he nor his party nor the majority of the public believe—such a view is supported neither by history, nor by the experience of the war itself, nor by common sense. For a minority to use the embarrassments of the war to impose any Socialist doctrine upon a doubting and reluctant majority, is not even going to promote Socialism. For there can be no widespread economic planning without stable political conditions, internally and externally. Socialism cannot be carried into fruitful social effect without an effective political instrument; without a bureaucracy that shall not be riven by deep doctrinal differences in addition to the normal bureaucratic jealousies.

The welding of thirty separate nations into an effective instrument of war and postwar organization is going to be difficult in any case. It is going to be impossible, if, in addition to securing agreement on the nature of their future political arrangements, they have to agree also upon the precise nature of the Socialism which they are to introduce.

For part of the trouble is that Socialists differ—deeply and sometimes bitterly—as to what Socialism really is. There are few things so productive of bitter argument. The Communists tell us it is one kind of thing to be achieved in one kind of way; various Socialist parties tell us, on the contrary, that it is something very different, to be achieved in a very different way. But even the Communists are not really agreed. In the last twenty years they have differed so much that in the home of Communism itself the government had to organize purges of the heretics, which threw millions of Russians either into concentration camps, prisons, or into Arctic exile, and involved indeed a widespread slaughter. So little agreed were Communists that one of their high priests, the close associate of Lenin, suffered banishment and finally death in exile for his differences with Stalin. To introduce such discordant elements is not going to facilitate the problem of a unified war effort, or a unified permanent defense afterwards; and if our purpose is to warn John Citizen of the reefs upon which unity might be wrecked there are facts here, dangers, of which he should be aware.

To clarify this relationship of the political to the economic problem is not to betray John to the capitalists; to "sell out to the bankers," or to be guilty of anything worse than stating the pretty obvious truth which John ought to know, to indicate the line of policy in international affairs which will give the best chance of that unity necessary for the defeat of Hitler; and resistance to future Hitlers.

A Note on the Social Revolution in Britain

In the case as presented by John Citizen in the first chapter of this book, two misgivings about the future are vigorously expressed. One is that any very close association with Great Britain in the post-war settlement may tie up this country with a Tory, imperialist, aristocratic system, incompatible with democratic aspirations and development. The other misgiving is that American radicals would utilize any close association with Britain to introduce a mass of "socialistic" planning along the lines of the British social securities system—with its dole, labor politics, a vast unemployment insurance scheme, and so forth.

Any day in America one may hear in conversation, or find expressed in the press, fear of both these mutually exclusive results of association with Britain. What is the truth about the social position of Britain?

The truth is that there has been great social advance underneath a great conservatism in outward forms—a conservatism very deceptive for foreigners, and even for some British. The social advance—which of course has not by any means been all that could have been wished, since big gaps have been left, might have been more rapid if some of the remaining relics of feudalism—monarchy, House of Lords, titles—had been swept completely away. But it is by no means certain. For the sweeping away of familiar forms, backed by feeling which attaches to things that have survived unnumbered generations, might have absorbed so much energy and caused so much friction that the reforms which really mattered might have been held up. The substance might have been sacrificed for the shadow. In any case a steady progress has been maintained peacefully, without severe internal strains; maintained while preserving the national unity. And, recalling what national unity has meant for the United Nations in the steadiness of British resistance to the Nazi onslaught, the sacrifice of some speed may have been justified.

It is obviously impossible to pass judgment on the points just discussed without some knowledge of what has actually been accomplished under the "gradualist" and Fabian method which has ruled in Britain. The facts of what has been accomplished in Britain under that method are astonishingly little known; and because they are exceedingly relevant to American problems, it is useful to add as an appendix to this chapter a brief review of the outstanding achievements. This review is based mainly on the work of Professor A. D. K. Owen of Glasgow University.

First of all, however, it is worth while taking note of two preliminary observations made by the German economist, Gustave Stolper. Dr. Stolper notes first of all:

The public outside England failed completely to realize what that country had quietly achieved in internal consolidation and modernization between the two World Wars. Criticism abroad ran in exactly the same ruts as if nothing at all had happened and Hitler's informants seemed to find comfort and reassurance in this lore. It may be doubted that British public opinion itself realized the greatness of the achievements in this era compared with those of the rest of the world. All these features of mature national effort we mention (and the many others we do not mention) account for the great historical miracle of our time: that in this Second World War Britain, alone and unprepared, has withstood assaults of organized chaos under which any lesser nation must have crumbled.

A further observation of Dr. Stolper deals with the British financial and commercial policy. He says:

To a much greater degree than in any other wealthy capitalist country, the private incomes derived from holdings of government bonds were received not by the rich but by the middle classes. The two decades between the wars saw an enormous growth of the middle classes and of small savings. While wage-earners received steadily about 40 per cent of the national income, salaries went up from 15.6 per cent in 1911 to 25 per cent in the 1930's. Correspondingly the share of property income declined. Of adults dying, 21 per cent left estates of over £100 in 1911–12, over 31 per cent left such twenty years later. With about the same number of owners, post-office savings rose from not quite £170,000,000 in 1910 to £390,000,000 in 1935, deposits in

Trustee Savings Banks from £55,000,000 to nearly £200,000,000. In the same quarter of a century the funds of Building Societies jumped from £62,000,000 to £571,000,000, those of Industrial and Provident Societies from £36,000,000 to more than £300,000,000. "The proletariat of the Marxist textbooks is fast disappearing." [4] Unless we realize how much Britain has become a middle-class country in the last two decades, how widely property has been dispersed, and how radically the inequality of wealth has been corrected, we cannot understand the essentially conservative climate of Britain's domestic policy.

The two means by which the fiscal policy achieved that end were the growing expansion of social services and the tax system. While £230,000,000 was required for the debt service, no less than £360,000,000 was devoted to various social services in the last years preceding the present war. Since 1929 alone these sums had been increased almost 20 per cent.

This was the fiscal policy of a Britain ruled by "an oligarchy of hereditary aristocrats, landowners, bankers, financiers and industrialists" to the detriment of the masses. While "in the United States income groups who had annual incomes of less than $3,000 accumulate in the aggregate practically no money savings," [5] we know from the studies of both Professor Bowley and Colin Clark that in Britain during the last two decades the rich as a class no longer made any contribution to national savings. For years the great estates in Britain have been in liquidation. It has been forced by huge estate and income taxes. Every year from 8 to 10 per cent of the peacetime budgets were drawn from estate duties. So confiscatory to large property were they that the feudalistic remnants would have died out with the present generation of owners had this war not occurred.

Appendix: A Note on Britain's Social Progress

Professor Owen in his monograph *The British Social Services* sketches the growth of the British Social Security System as follows:

---

[4] E. F. M. Durbin, *The Politics of Democratic Socialism*, Routledge, London, 1940.

[5] Temporary National Economic Committee, *Monograph* No. 25, p. 29.

The new century opened up a new epoch in the development of the public social services, and the period between 1906 and the Great War produced a rich crop of social legislation. A generation ahead of its American counterpart, it was indeed a "New Deal" for the British working class. In 1906 local education authorities were given powers to provide free meals for necessitous schoolchildren. In the following year a school medical service was set up. Thirty years of zealous advocacy by social reformers culminated in the introduction of non-contributory old-age pensions in 1908. A national system of employment exchanges and the first Town Planning Act came in 1909. Trade Boards, for the determination of legally enforceable minimum wages and working conditions for those engaged in certain badly organised industries, were established in the same year. In 1911 two important social insurance schemes—national health and unemployment insurance—were established, and the first steps were taken to create an adequate tuberculosis service. Two years later an important measure relating to the treatment of mental deficiency was passed.

During the last war a public service for the prevention and treatment of venereal disease was established, and a far-reaching measure of educational reform was introduced in 1918. Maternity and child-welfare services, which had been provided by some municipalities and voluntary organisations for many years, were widely extended after the war and, in 1920, the arrangements for looking after the welfare of the blind were greatly improved. During the next twenty years unemployment and the housing problem were the chief preoccupations of the social welfare departments of the State. Unemployment insurance was extended to cover about two-thirds of the wage-earning population and, after a great deal of trial and error, an unemployment assistance service was set up in 1934 to provide for workers who were outside the scope of unemployment insurance or who had exhausted their insurance rights. A long series of Housing Acts were passed during this period, and a great deal of activity has taken place as a result. Over four and a half million new houses have been built, most of them of the type required by working-class families, and several hundred thousand slum houses have been demolished. One-third of the entire population of Great Britain has been re-housed since 1918. Meanwhile a contributory pensions scheme has been introduced for widows, orphans, and insured workers and their wives over 65, and considerable extensions and improvements in the health services have taken place. The outbreak of war in September 1939 appeared to destroy all hope of further expansion of the social services for the time being. In March 1940, however, an Act was passed providing contributory old-age pensions for insured women and the wives of insured men at the age of 60, and supplementary pensions for all old-age pensioners who establish their need for them. Moreover, the war has led to the development of several new forms of voluntary social service—such as clubs and welfare activities for children evacuated from dangerous areas to the safe countryside, and Citizens' Advice Bureaux to help people with wartime problems and difficulties.

The British public social services which are in operation today may be conveniently grouped under four general headings. There are, in the first place, a number of services which have been described as constructive community services. These services include education, the public health and medical services, the national system of employment exchanges, and the arrangements for looking after the welfare of the blind, the mental defective, the insane, and other subnormal members of the community. In each case the service takes the form of providing specialised institutions and professional skill for common use. Public authorities provide schools and teachers, hospitals, clinics, sanatoria, doctors, nurses, and health visitors; employment exchanges and employment officers; workshops and clubs, instructors and welfare workers for blind people, and so on. They are essentially constructive services, for their purpose is to improve individual fitness and the social adaptation of the persons with whom they deal. They may be fairly described as community services because they are not restricted to any particular social class. Most well-to-do people may still prefer to send their children to private schools, to go to private nursing homes, and to use private employment exchanges, but they are not barred from using the public services, and, in point of fact, as these services have improved in quality the number of middle-class people who use their facilities has greatly increased.

The second group of services may be described as forms of subsidised consumption. Certain essentials of civilised life—healthy and

properly equipped homes and some vital elements in diet—cannot
be obtained by many citizens with low incomes owing to their high
cost at ordinary market prices. Modern standards of housing, which
assume the need for at least three or four rooms, in addition to a
kitchen and bathroom, for a wage-earner's family, involve high rents
if costs are to be met, and the minimum dietaries prescribed by modern physiologists for young and growing children and for expectant
and nursing mothers are frequently too expensive for the lower-paid
workers' families. The difficulty can, however, be met by the payment of public subsidies, and these have, in fact, been paid on a
large scale during the last twenty years to make it possible to
re-house millions of wage-earners and their dependants in new gar-
den estates and modern flats, and to enable mothers and children to
obtain milk and other food at prices within their means. During the
present war the Government has extended this principle to meet the
need to keep down the price of certain essential articles of food,
such as bread, meat, and milk, and considerable sums are now being
devoted to this purpose.[6]

The third group of services consists of the social insurances. These
services—which include unemployment and health insurance and the
widows', orphans', and old-age contributory pensions scheme—may
be regarded as a system of compulsory self-help, organised by the
State and subsidised by the taxpayer and by employers of labour.
Manual workers, and salaried employees earning not more than 250
pounds,[7] are required by law to make regular weekly contributions to
a fund, to which their employers and the State also contribute, and
from which they receive specific benefits in the event of unemployment, sickness, or disability, widowhood, orphanhood, or old age.
The social insurances are the principal bulwark of the working-class
population of Great Britain against poverty due to a failure of earnings from employment. Securely based upon a well-understood and
generally accepted principle of mutual insurance, generously under-

---

[6] During the early months of 1940 the cost of the public subsidies for this
purpose amounted to over 1 million pounds a week. Milk is now supplied at
half price to all expectant and nursing mothers and to children under 5, and
is supplied free in all cases of poverty.

[7] The unemployment insurance scheme was extended in June 1940 to cover
"black-coated" workers earning not more than 420 pounds.

written by the taxpayer, they are unmistakably popular, and the political representatives of organised labour are committed to their extension in various directions. Workmen's compensation insurance is not included among the British public social services. Employers are legally liable to pay compensation, and most of them insure against this risk either with commercial insurance companies or through their own associations. The present arrangements are not regarded as being satisfactory, and a Royal Commission is now investigating the whole question.

The fourth group consists of social services which provide assistance for those whose needs are not covered by social insurance benefits. These social assistance services include non-contributory old-age pensions payable at the age of 70; supplementary pensions payable to old-age pensioners whose needs are not wholly covered by the standard rate of pension; unemployment assistance allowances; and poor relief, under its modern name, public assistance. All of these services have two things in common—they are financed wholly out of public funds raised by taxation (national taxation in the case of pensions and unemployment assistance, local taxation in the case of poor relief), and, in each case, some account is taken, in granting assistance, of the financial circumstances of the applicant. Of these services, non-contributory old-age pensions payable at 70 stand in a separate class from the others, as the "means test" which is imposed on applicants for these pensions is extremely liberal and no account is taken of the income of other members of their families. On the other hand, supplementary old-age pensions, unemployment allowances, and public assistance are not granted until the authorities have investigated the applicants' household resources and determined the extent of the need.

Another way of estimating the importance of the public social services is to consider the part which they play in the life of a typical working-class family. When a young wage-earner marries he may be fortunate enough to rent a house on a municipal estate at rent reduced to the extent of several shillings a week by means of a public subsidy. Before his first child is born his wife will be wise to visit an ante-natal clinic at an infant welfare centre or maternity hospital. The birth may well take place at a public maternity home or hospital, or the child may be delivered at home by a midwife on the staff of the local health authority. In any event, the baby will be visited by a "health visitor," and this will probably be followed by attendance at an infant welfare centre, where the baby will be weighed and examined and where the mother will have an opportunity of obtaining advice and help and, if need be, milk and other foods free or at reduced prices. There is no reason why the mother should not continue to attend the welfare centre until the child is 5, though if she is fortunate enough to be living near a nursery school or a nursery class she would do well to take advantage of an opportunity which is still unhappily rare.

When the child is 5 the time comes for attendance at an ordinary school. Here the child will not only be educated but also medically examined and treated for minor ailments by a school doctor or nurse. Meanwhile the ill-health or unemployment of the child's father may have given rise to claims for health and unemployment insurance benefits and, possibly, if ill-health or unemployment has been prolonged, to an application for unemployment assistance or poor relief. An industrial accident or disease would probably involve treatment in hospital, and would, in any case, give rise to a claim under the Workmen's Compensation Acts. If the wage earner dies, his widow will be entitled to a pension for herself and an allowance for her children until they reach the age of 16. On the other hand, if both of them live, they may look forward to old-age pensions when the husband is 65 and the wife 60 years old. If these pensions—10s. per week each—are insufficient for their needs, it will be possible for them to obtain supplementary pensions under the new scheme which has come into force in 1940. The example which has been taken is not unusual. It is broadly true to the life of millions of British working-class families, and it illustrated how continuously and intimately the public social services affect the lives of ordinary citizens in this country today.

It is important to notice that no social stigma attaches to participation in the benefits of any of these services. Even the poor law in its modern form—public assistance—has lost most of its earlier unhappy associations, and it no longer carries with it civil disabilities for those whom it benefits. By and large, the public social services are accepted as sensible and businesslike collective arrangements for meeting the social needs of the ordinary citizen. Collective provision, whether in the field of education, of health, or of social insurance, is recognised as being more economical than any other arrangement, and the evils of bureaucracy are kept at bay by the vigilance of democratically elected representatives of the people, by public criticism in a free press, and by the participation of voluntary organisations and voluntary workers in social service administration. Under a totalitarian system the social services may be, as indeed they are in some countries, used as instruments for creating a servile mentality. In Great Britain they are the jealously guarded responsibilities of scores of democratic bodies and of tens of thousands of public-spirited citizens.[8]

---

[8] Reprinted from *The British Social Services* by A. D. K. Owen, by permission of the author, the British Council, and the publishers, Longmans, Green Ltd.

If this is to be truly "the people's war" then we must keep it the war of all the people, not merely some. If the United Nations are to remain united, even for the purposes of the war, we must become more conscious of the impelling moral basis of unity, our criticisms must be of policies, not of each other, ancient grudges must be sacrificed; and "natural" tribal instincts made subject to adult discipline.

CHAPTER VI

The Unity of the Peoples

IF THIS book has a single text, it is that two wars have come upon us in a single generation because we have forgotten the elementary social truth that the right of each to life must be defended collectively, by the community, or it cannot be defended at all; that if we will not defend the rights of others against violence we shall at last be unable to defend our own and will ourselves become the victims of that violence. If within the nation the people as a whole are indifferent when some minority is made the victim of gross violence; if in the international field the nations as a whole are indifferent when some one people is the victim of such violence, then the rights of all the people and of all peoples are placed in jeopardy.

Here surely is a truth which lies at the heart of democracy and is of its essence. No one is likely to challenge it so long as it is stated abstractly—and vaguely. But as soon as any precision at all is given to it, those who are sometimes most clamant and noisy in espousing "the cause of the people," challenge it fundamentally.

The very terms of the proposition that to defend our own rights we must defend those of others means that with rights go certain obligations, certain duties, and that by the fulfillment of those obligations alone can the rights be defended; that failing the performance of the duties, by the people, their rights will be destroyed and perish.

In attempting to find, in the case of the nations of Europe, why this indispensable condition of the effective defense of popular rights, of freedom, was neglected, we make very early this discovery: the great masses are unaware of these duties, of the defensive interdependence of groups and of nations. The history of the popular movements within both France and Germany is illuminating in this connection.

Germany, the fatherland of Marx, had before 1914 a tradition of struggle for the rights of the workers, and had produced a vast literature of the subject, powerful organizations, a great workers' press, powerful trade-unions. The preaching of the social revolution and class war was carried on with an energy far greater than that given to the doctrine in Britain or America. And the net effect of it all, if we are to judge by results, was to create, not a sense of the solidarity of the German people and a capacity of political co-operation, but such a tendency to factions and parties that the people were incapable of resisting the domination of a Hitler prepared to play off one group against another. Always were the differences of doctrine stressed, conflicts of interest as compared with any identity of interest enlarged upon; always, therefore, was there a greater readiness to find an enemy than an ally; always insistence upon the inevitability of class conflict; the impossibility of agreement or compromise with other groups.

The people of France, for all their long revolutionary tradition, were betrayed into slavery—whether to Hitler or Laval—partly by some similar difficulty in agreeing who were the people, how their unity and solidarity could be maintained. In many countries in Europe—and elsewhere—one found before the war a multiplicity of political parties, each convinced that it alone stood for the "cause of the people." But so often one found also, on examination, that Jews or Communists or Catholics, or members of the bourgeoisie, or employers, or capitalists or Social Democrats or Mensheviks or Social Revolutionaries, or Socialists, or Negroes, were not by one or other of these parties considered "the people."

We now face the problem of organizing the people, and the peoples, for freedom.

Upon what large common interest can that world-wide co-operation be based? Who are "the people" or "the common people"? Goebbels has just been reminding us (he is frequently doing it) that Hitler is "a man of the common people" and that Franklin Roosevelt is not, but comes of a group of old, rich, and distinguished American families typical of the pluto-democracies. Goebbels might have enlarged on the comparison. Mussolini is "a man of the common people." He has frequently talked of his blacksmith-peasant origin. Churchill is an aristocrat, grandson of a duke, a descendant of the famous Duke of Marlborough. Stalin is a man of the people. But Lenin, who made the Russian revolution and made Stalin possible, was not. Lincoln was "a man of the people." But he adopted a profession which would have made him "bourgeois" in Russia, where he would probably have been liquidated in the early purges. The most radical man in the British Cabinet, the Socialist Cripps, is the son of a British peer. His colleague in the Cabinet, the much less radical Bevin, is the son of a day laborer, and has spent most of his life defending the interests of dock workers. These purely personal facts would have no political importance were it not for misconceptions that have gathered about certain very current terms.

When we insist that this is a "people's war," a war of the "common people," whom do we exclude? Who are outside that category? The frequency with which the term is used seems to imply that it is not the war of some section of the population. That on the one side stand "the common people," anxious to wage this war, with a great stake in it, and on the other certain sections not so anxious to wage it, with no great stake in it, yet, it is commonly implied, responsible for it.

Many who admit that this may not be a very true picture seem to imply that it is an inaccuracy that does not particularly matter, since insistence upon it may add to the morale of the underprivileged, who might otherwise feel that they had no great stake in the struggle. It has been fashionable of recent years in Left circles to insist that every war is a class war, brought about by the capitalist or possessing class as a means of promoting their class interest; and that this war represents a struggle of the "common people" against an old order of class domination. As we saw in the last chapter, some writers, both in Britain and America, demand that if the war is not already, it should now be made, a "revolutionary war" waged for the purpose of introducing their conception of Socialism.

For some time now the claim has been made that the war cannot be won under the leadership of men or parties associated with or committed to the preservation of the old order of private property, or private enterprise. The claim is, to put it in the somewhat crude terms of some British critics, that only a government of convinced and orthodox Socialists can hope to lead the peoples to victory.

Although the present writer is himself a Socialist, he does not believe this to be true; or that it indicates a sound policy likely to secure the largest measure of unity among the United Nations, without which there can be no victory likely to embody the largest measure of common interest.

Why the Churchill Leadership?

Certain facts in this connection may usefully be recalled. When Britain was so near to defeat after Dunkerque that some of the best military minds in the world were of the opinion that she could not possibly hold out further, the British people were rallied by a leadership which will make one of the greatest stories of democratic leadership in all history. The world had witnessed the collapse of France by reason of deep internal divisions—a revolutionary Socialism (evidenced by the presence of over seventy Communist deputies in the Chamber of Deputies) confronting a reactionary bourgeoisie more concerned to grasp at the chance of saving, by a shameful surrender, what remained of their possessions, than to risk them by continuing the war from Africa. Was Britain to reveal the same internal divisions, the same betrayal?

To what manner of man did Britain—that is to say the British people, the population of the islands—turn in that hour? They did not turn to a revolutionary Socialist, to one who promised a new order (he promised indeed nothing but blood and sweat and toil and tears). They could hardly have turned to a revolutionary Socialist, for at that moment the strongest Socialist forces of the world as represented by Russia and her Communist allies in the various countries were opposed to any continuation of the war against Germany. Russia was at the time allied by a peace pact with Germany and the slogan of revolutionary Communism the world over was that this was just another imperialist war, with which "the people" had no concern,—or had no other concern than to bring it to an end as rapidly as possible; if necessary by sabotage of the war effort, while Russia supplied material for the German war machine.

In the United States, not merely the Communists, but a large part of the non-Communist Left, the Socialist Party, notably its leader, also took the line that the struggle against Germany was just a war of rival imperialisms, and that the sooner it was brought to an end, even if it meant the defeat of Britain, the better. The Communists in Britain itself then took the view that it was an imperialist war and were either failing to support it or were actively opposing its prosecution. Had their influence been greater, had leadership in Britain been then at that date of a kind which depended upon Communist support, the outcome might have been a "negotiated" peace. Britain would have followed in the footsteps of France—as indeed nearly everyone outside Britain supposed that she would be compelled to do. Had she done so, the world would have been delivered to Hitler and his allies.

What followed in that year during which Britain, with the greater part of her equipment lost in France, was obliged to arm many of her people with sporting rifles and shot guns, terrifyingly out-numbered in the air, her airmen day after day without proper rest or sleep facing odds of three, four, at times ten to one—all that is now a familiar story.

It was at a time when, for many an English worker during months on end, the forty-hour week became an eighty, ninety, and hundred-hour week; when men slept by their machines in their work clothes, and woke to go on with the work, while death rained overhead; when children and old women stood fire watch on the roof and perished in burning buildings they had defended.

What was the inspiration? And what lay behind the leadership? This present writer has no complete answer. But he wants to eliminate false answers, that cannot help us now and in the future. It is no complete answer merely to say "patriotism." The French had patriotism too. At that date the inspiration cannot possibly have been that of the "class war," of revolutionary Socialism, at a time, that is, when Russia, the very Mecca of the revolutionary Socialist, was in virtual alliance with Germany, and Communists the world over were doing their best to achieve cessation of the war against the Nazi power. All parties have testified to the strange command which Churchill at that moment had over the minds and hearts of the British people; over virtually all of them. The Socialist Labour Party accepted his leadership; the Tories and Liberals accepted it; all accepted it. During that crucial year, when everything hung upon British unity, the nation found in this Tory aristocrat the embodiment of its purpose, its aims. He was trusted, not merely as a military commander, a strategist (probably today a good many regard his military quality as his least) but as the nation's natural leader, expressing its attitude, its outlook, its loyalties, its scale of values. Can we say of such a man who personifies, as few have ever done, the very soul of a people, that he makes no part of that people? There is surely something nonsensical, comically false, in the suggestion that when we speak of the "people" of England, the "British people," we must not include the Churchills.[1]

Nor will it make for that unity which the United Nations must find and keep, or perish, to say that the Churchills (or for that mat-

---

[1] Marcel Hoden, the French writer, commented in 1940:
Between him and the people there grew a kind of mysterious link, a deep and constant communion, such as history seldom shows between a great warrior and his army, or a statesman and the nation whose destiny is in his care. In the hour of extreme danger, they knew he was there, keeping watch day and night; they knew his only thought was for resistance, his only care for the organization of the forces. They watched for the almost legendary figure of the thick-set fighter, they waited upon his words of praise or blame or of comfort. He shared the joys and the sufferings of all and he knew how to express them in magnificent language which made hearts beat faster. He was the embodiment of the fight to the finish, of confidence, hope and the will to live and to conquer. He was the very soul of the nation.

ter the Roosevelts) cannot be considered as truly part of the struggle unless and until they have embraced some particular form of Socialism; and that the moral values which made it possible for a Churchill to lead, and a whole people to give him their support, make no part of the things for which we fight.

The truth is that though Churchill may in some of his policies stand for interests which conflict with other interests, he stands also for some interests which are the common interests of the whole people. Those interests are the fundamental ones.

The Moral Basis of Unity

Certainly John Citizen is right to insist that we do much better in the future than we have done in the past in the matter of social reform; that whatever we can do for war we should insist shall be done for the purposes of peace. All that is legitimate, wise, helpful.

But to go on from there and to tell John Citizen (who very often does not belong to the proletariat at all, who more often than not is dominated by the despised "middle-class psychology") that the bourgeoisie, all those who compose the business world, are his enemies, that they are thinking of nothing but their profits, that to win the war they must be liquidated and the whole nation must embrace the doctrine of Socialism (when there is deep disagreement as to what the doctrine is and how best to apply it)—is to tell him something which, first, is not true, second, is denied by experience, and third, would be calculated to defeat the coming of any new order which is at once both Socialist and free since it would add to the forces of disintegration by which the Nazi enemy has already profited far too much.

What John is fighting for is the right to demand from his government Socialism or anything else that he wants or would like to try, without having that right denied either by outside power or power within the state set up by the help of outside power. And the problem now is to put the military purpose first, to see that our effort is not divided and that we don't fall between several elusive stools.

Nothing is easier to secure than agreement upon the desirability of unity; nothing more difficult to determine than the concessions of doctrine or conviction which each should make in order to secure that unity. It is quite clear that if nobody is to make any concession whatever, if no one is willing even to postpone the enforcement of his views, then there can be no unity at all.

The dangers are obvious enough. On the Left there are passionate convictions that the war should be made the occasion for the complete abolition of the existing economic system now. The tendency of much comment is to create the impression that such a change is resisted, not from any conviction which comes of putting the war effort first, but from a selfish desire to protect vested interests. It has repeatedly been suggested that the delay in opening a second front is not due to military considerations, but to anti-Russian prejudice on the part of those directing operations, due to fears of a complete Russian victory. That sort of debate clearly tends to make public decision on strategic questions a matter of political and ideological passion and partisanship. Into other decisions enter prepossessions of another order. There is widespread American conviction that Indian unity and fighting morale would be immediately promoted by yielding to the demands of the Congress Party in India. The British objection that this would provoke bitter opposition on the part of the Moslems and have dangerous repercussions throughout the Moslem world is ascribed to the desire of imperialists to retain power in India with a view to the postwar period. In both cases there enter into vital war decisions class, doctrinal, and nationalist differences which ought to be absent.

Obviously, if we are to get unity at all some convictions must be held in abeyance; and the old nationalist grudges ended for good.

The greatest danger perhaps at this stage to the unity of Allied strategy and a unified command, is the liability to Anglo-American squabbling, usually squabbling over trifles.

The insistence in these pages upon the need for a unity sufficient for effective co-operation between the United Nations, does not imply the advocacy of any particular political machinery or constitutional form of co-operation. The fact that the nations of the British Commonwealth—Canada, Australia, New Zealand, South Africa—stood with Britain at the very outbreak of the war (as in the previous World War) though they had the right to stand aside, is proof that no very tight constitutional ties or federalism are necessary for effective co-operation. If the Geneva League failed, it was not so much from constitutional defect (though it was defective) as from the failure of its members to fulfill their obligations to support each other against aggression as effectively as the members of the British League or Commonwealth of Nations fulfilled their obligations. Yet in the latter case there were no legal or statutory compulsions at all. The will to act in common proved more important than any elaborate prearranged way of doing it. If the Geneva League failed it was because so many of those who composed it (and of those who remained outside) did not really want a League at all, however good its constitution.

This present writer is not one of those who believe that the best way to secure peace and freedom is for the English-speaking nations—the United States and the British Commonwealth—to dominate the world or impose their own judgment upon it. None should dominate; all should accept the domination of the law against violence, which all should support. But I do believe that we shall not get that world law, that there can be no peace or freedom, if the English-speaking nations are weak and divided. If the United States and Britain quarrel, then the United Nations cannot remain united. If we, America and Britain, cannot work together, who can? English-speaking unity and co-operation are not, of themselves, sufficient; but they are indispensable. There must be more than English-speaking co-operation. But if that goes, all goes. Of course, we may abuse our power. But the remedy for that danger is not to be found in both of us being weak. That would only confront us with new dangers. The remedy is to see that our power be used as the means by which others shall enjoy the rights we demand for ourselves.

The question of Anglo-American disagreement will become more acute as the association of the two governments becomes closer, and the number of common problems to be solved greater. Both peoples have a deeply rooted habit of free criticism of government; but criticism of decisions made in common by the two governments will easily become criticism of one government by the people of the other country. Senatorial criticism of Britain's policy in India, and an implied demand that Britain grant India immediate freedom is a case in point.

One's first instinct is to say, "Let there be no criticism on either side when a common policy has been agreed upon!" But that is hardly feasible. Both peoples have too long a tradition of extremely free criticism in their politics and public life. No man in English public life, for many generations, has won the degree of affection and regard today shown by the British people for Winston Churchill. Yet during a great part of this year he has had to face bitter, sometimes ferocious criticism, in the House of Commons; criticism mainly of his conduct as Minister of Defense, as the responsible head of Britain's military operations. Tomorrow, in order to get completely unified command, the responsibility may pass to Franklin Roosevelt. In that case there will certainly at times be criticism of Roosevelt's policy in the House of Commons, just as there has been of Churchill's. It is difficult to see how this can be avoided. The armies, navies, and resources of one country may be under the command and direction of men of the other, just as Australia's forces are now under the command of an American. The public forces of the British Empire may be under the control and command of an American president, in the sense that he may head the Supreme Council. Is there to be no criticism at all by the representatives of the British whom, in that event, President Roosevelt commands? An American friend, when the implications of this development toward a unified command were pointed out, said: "The House of Commons will just have to keep its trap shut." If that is really necessary, many an Englishman will feel that the bottom has fallen out of democracy. A grievance which can find no free expression is likely to become what, with plentiful airing, it need never become, dangerous and explosive.

Mere silence, hiding this problem in the cellar, is not a possible solution. The solution is to accept certain moral implications of the term "United Nations," and to realize that, unless the very basis of democracy is to be surrendered in our search for unity, we must somehow manage to make unity compatible with tolerant discussion, with decent criticism.

It is because of such possibilities that I have not hesitated in these pages to discuss frankly but objectively, the problem of Anglophobia on the one side and "British superciliousness" and certain grave defects of British policy on the other. It is surely better that defects should be explained. The subject is generally regarded as "dangerous." But you don't solve problems by running away from them; and if this is a real problem—which even those most afraid of discussing it insist it is—then the best plan is to drag it into the light and see what there is in it; a process which usually reveals the fact that there is not as much in it as we feared, and that it was mainly our fears of tackling it which made it a problem.

The problem of Allied unity is mainly one of Anglo-American unity in the sense already indicated; not that such unity is all-sufficient, but that it is indispensable to any larger unity. Nor is the main danger that of complete and permanent rupture. This will not take place. But what may take place are disastrous delays in the taking of indispensable steps because of difficulty in agreeing that they are the best steps, or necessary. The outcome of this war—whether it be a four- or five-year war or a ten-year war—will depend, not merely upon what we do, but upon when we do it.

It is merely fatuous to pretend that there will be no friction when an immense American army is quartered in Britain, paid at a much higher scale than British soldiers, with luxuries and rations such as the British have not seen since the war began; not subject to British law or British courts in the case of offenses against British citizens, but by a special law subject only to American courts operating on British soil. Fortunately the American authorities are facing the facts of life and are taking suitable measures. The "notes" issued by the War Department for the guidance of American soldiers in

Britain are admirable, and should prove of real use in preventing trouble. Other educational efforts are being undertaken. If both sides proceed on the assumption, *not* that friction and disagreement would be so wicked that we must not speak or think or do anything about it, but proceed on the contrary assumption that there will certainly be grave conflict unless we do something about it, unless there is organized educational effort to prevent it, then we can prevent it.

Nor should the policy of facing the facts and meeting them by educational discipline be confined to the soldiers.

Ever since the beginning of the war it has been a perfectly obvious fact that the opponents of the President's foreign policy have seized upon Anglophobia, wherever they could find it, as a very convenient political weapon. Anglophobia has served the demagogue in America and in some degree in France, somewhat (though to nothing like the same extent) as anti-Semitism served the demagogue in Germany. Just as Hitler used anti-Semitism (the charge that the country had been captured by the Jews) as a convenient club wherewith to help in beating the Weimar Republic to death; so certain isolationists have found Anglophobia, the charge that "the British have moved into the White House," a convenient weapon wherewith to fight the foreign policy of the President.[2]

A subsequent chapter deals more fully with the nature of such phenomenon as anti-Semitism and nationalist grudges maintained much as the old hillbillies maintained mountain feuds. It is relevant at this stage to insist that these diseases of the human soul *are* subject to educational and spiritual treatment. Certain ignorances exacerbate them and to dispel those ignorances makes the "instinct"

---

[2] "To say that Roosevelt's foreign policy out-Hoovers Hoover would be going too far. Hoover's was unique; Roosevelt's is merely typical in its devotion to British interests.

"If American neutrality policy runs counter to British interests, it will be rewritten to conform with them; likewise, if American devotion to the democratic principle inconveniences the British Foreign Office, on that score too Mr. Roosevelt will accommodate himself to Britain's convenience."—From *Britain Expects Every American to Do His Duty*, by Quincy Howe (pp. 44–45).

to quarrel more manageable. (Thus the purpose of the chapter which follows this.)

A Note on Group Animosities

The main factor in these frictions is the innate tendency of all of us to resent anything which is "different" and doesn't belong to our tribe, our club, our church, our village, our nation, our race. The English psychologist, Trotter, has described this as the herd instinct. Other psychologists have told us that there is no such thing as the herd instinct. But what we do know from everyday experience is that there is a very deep tendency to divide up into groups, to make divisions based on any mortal thing—religious belief, color of the hair, shape of the nose, place of residence. Having made these divisions we naturally place our group ahead of other groups. Of course, we, whatever the way may be, are the superior people, the Herrenvolk, the chosen people. Why shouldn't we be? It gives us a sense of nice superiority, of exclusiveness, of being in the Social Register.

As a child in England, I recall that on that March day when Oxford and Cambridge row their boat races, the children of the village where I lived always wore colors showing whether they were Oxford or Cambridge, and, although I am quite sure few of us knew what a boat race was, and none of us knew what a university was, by the end of the day our mutual taunts had led us to pummeling each other, and the light blues had become convinced that the dark blues were despicable folk, if not the enemies of mankind. It is perfectly easy to invent a race out of nothing, as Hitler has done in the case of the Aryans, and on this nonexistent basis to create deep and deadly hatreds. Perhaps the deadliest hatreds have been over the religious differences.

All this, of course, belongs to the irrational element in us. But perhaps the great mistake that we have made in our ideas of education and upbringing is to assume that we can do nothing about it.

If you cannot change human nature, you can change human behavior, which is what matters. Much of history is, indeed, a record of the way in which human behavior has been changed. And behavior sets up a habit. And habit is, as we know, second nature. Indeed modern psychologists tell us now that it is largely first nature. In any case you can change it.

Some years ago, in a British cinema, someone raised the cry of "Fire." The audience obeyed their instinct, their nature, the instinct of self-preservation, which, of all instincts, is, I suppose, one of the most deep-rooted. They made a rush for the doors; there was a bad jam and several people were trampled to death. There was no fire. It was a false alarm.

A few days later, in another theater, once more the cry of "Fire" was raised. The manager happened to be present and was determined that there should be no such tragedy in his house. He jumped to the stage and shouted with the loudest voice he could command to the crowd to keep their seats. He told them there was plenty of time and that they knew what they had to do: to look for the nearest exit, rise, walk quietly. That theater was emptied in perfect order, although this time there was a fire and the place was burned to the ground.

Were you dealing with a different human nature in the second case? Of course you were not. You were dealing with precisely the same kind of human beings as in the first case. But the behavior in the second was entirely different because, by the happy intervention of the manager, the first thought was made subject to the second thought. The people were reminded to discipline themselves.

And this it would seem is what we ought to do in the presence of this national prejudice. We know that it results in evil behavior, in wrong policies which produce infinite misery and torment. We know also that it is largely irrational, based, as in the case of alleged Aryan superiority, on mere suggestion, a suggestion which in that case every educated man in the world, including every man who teaches it in Germany, knows to be ignorant nonsense.

As we all have to live together in this very small world of ours whether we are of different races or not; and as we cannot create and maintain a decent civilization without ever-closer co-operation, surely our social sciences should be taught in such a way as to convey to us a warning of the traps into which we shall fall if we are not made aware of them. It is said commonly that moral exhortation does very little to change human behavior. But the moral values which we acquire, our sense of what is important and what unimportant, what noble, what good, what bad—these conceptions, which are very much the result of talk, discussion, literature, do infinitely affect behavior. It is time that our education in the social sciences, our learning of history (which might well begin with some notion of anthropology), undertook to make us aware of dangers against which we must prepare ourselves by the relevant disciplines. We shall never become properly educated for democracy until we cease fulsomely to flatter our vanity by saying that "the voice of the people is the voice of God." That is exactly equivalent to saying that whatever we do collectively, whatever prejudice, pugnacity, quarrelsomeness we indulge, must be right. Let us honestly face the fact that we do all commit errors, that our instincts and pugnacities do at times lead us astray; that the voice of the people is sometimes the voice of Satan, and that we can best serve mankind at times by calling attention to the fact.

Perhaps the gravest risks to the unity of the United Nations today arise from misunderstandings due to distortion of our thought by certain very current words whose meaning we have not examined. What does "owning" an empire mean? If the United States were to take over all the British Empire, would any John Citizen in America own anything he does not now possess? The power of words is such that they have prevented our learning some of the most important events in the world's history. We cannot understand what MacArthur is doing in Australia, nor what America should do in the future, nor how the task of political reconstruction can be carried out unless we know a little more of what has been happening within the British "Empire"; what it really is, how it could be used in the tasks ahead.

CHAPTER VII

Words That Are Assassins

VERY nearly half the questions raised by John Citizen in the first chapter of this book have some reference to the British Empire and British imperialism. Why are Americans now fighting in defense of an empire against which their forefathers rebelled, and would have done their best to destroy? Was not the last peace ruined by the British imperialists? Does not Britain own far too much? Is not Lindbergh right when he says that the fundamental cause of this war is that "Britain owns too much of the world and Germany too little?" Is it not a gross injustice that a people numbering some forty-five million should own a quarter of the earth? And much more to the same effect.

Throughout these questions there runs an undercurrent of suspicion, obviously based, in John's view on past record, that when the time for settlement comes, Britain will pull a fast one.

Behind this persistent suspicion have lain two main facts: a failure to give full account of the forces which really explain the expansion of a state placed as Britain has been placed; but, in addition to that, the vast misapprehension which has arisen from the persistent use of words and terms which are so inaccurate as utterly to distort clear thought. This second point will be dealt with presently. Let us take now the first.

The chapter which follows this attempts to show that in an anarchistic world, where each is dependent for survival solely upon his own individual power, a nation will find itself again and again confronted with this stark alternative: conquer, or be conquered. Repeatedly does this struggle for power, as the only means of self-preservation, compel it to occupy a given territory (as the United

States is occupying Iceland, Greenland, and other territory) or see it occupied and its position and resources used by an enemy.

A nation cannot be asked to commit suicide on behalf of the higher morality. No nation would in fact adopt that course. We cannot therefore count it a sin that a nation should have expanded the area of its domination. (The United States itself is one of the great examples in history of territorial expansion.) What we can in justice condemn is a failure to accord equality of right as between conqueror and conquered; a failure to turn domination into partnership; to allow a relationship of "status" to become one of "contract."

That Britain in the eighteenth century should have pushed France out of Canada (and as part of the same world-wide struggle out of India as well) was perhaps an inevitable part of the defense of the English colonies in America, and of Britain's position generally. If British power had not been so exercised the United States might never have come into being. It would indeed be barren to discuss the moral merits of that particular conflict. But in estimating whether the power so established can be considered as a factor of order, right, freedom, democracy, throughout the world, we have to examine how the imperial power is being used; whether to perpetuate domination or to ensure equality of right as between all the various elements.

If the advice of some anti-imperialists had been adopted and Brittain had simply evacuated all imperially held territory—Gibraltar, Malta, Aden, Egypt—the world today would be in Hitler's hands. This does not mean that all imperialism is justifiable or that all imperialisms are alike; and that success will justify any. The position of Australia or New Zealand in the British "empire" is not really similar to that of Poland in the German New Order. The difference is not merely that of relative "severity." The difference is that under the British "imperial" system Britain so modified her position that today she has no authority whatever within the territory of Australia or Canada or any other Dominion. She can make no law for any of these territories. In other words the imperial authority has disappeared and been replaced by the free partnership of equals, bound together for defensive purposes by the loosest possible understanding, a sort of gentleman's agreement that an attack on one member of this particular league of nations would be regarded as an attack on all. And this league worked where the Geneva League failed, mainly, as a system of collective security.

If instead of this evolution, the whole system had simply been allowed to disintegrate as a piece of political wickedness, the result would have been neither freedom nor security: for the fight against Hitler could not have been maintained.

What is to be the future course of development of the British and Dutch Empires? Are they to disintegrate into independencies? What, in that case, of the defense of territories in the Far East which, undefended save by the power of each independent state acting separately, would be certain to fall into the hands of more powerful neighbors and restart once more the competition for power? What of access to raw materials?

Even more important than these questions of the future, are the possibilities of disagreements between the United Nations likely to arise if the basic facts of the situation are misunderstood. And much misunderstanding does already exist owing to the use of words which, to the mind of one carries one meaning and to another something entirely different. ("Empire" itself is one such word.)

"There stalk about among us," said Ruskin on one occasion, "certain masked words. They sow terror, they bribe, they beguile. And no man asks what lies behind the mask. They acquire such power that they become the unjust stewards of men's minds, so that at last no man's mind can be reached save through their evil ministry."

When Colonel Lindbergh declared that the fundamental cause of the present war lay in the fact that Britain owned too much of the world and Germany too little, many American newspapers and commentators took him severely to task on one ground or another. But the implication of much of the criticism was along the line that this was not the time to point out facts which figured so prominently in the propaganda of Mr. Goebbels; and that though it might be wrong for Britain to own a quarter of the earth, better Britain than the Nazis.

Not one of these critics, so far as I am aware, pointed out that Colonel Lindbergh (like thousands of others in every country, including Britain) was using a word which in this context could not possibly, on any careful examination, be true in its ordinary meaning. Yet because so many men are careless in the use of language, that word would be accepted in its ordinary meaning as true even in that context; and by that fact an utterly false picture would become fixed in the minds of millions, a picture which simply parts company with all reality and fact; which gives rise to bitterness and resentment and perpetuates myths and fantasies that make clear thought about the facts—difficult and complex enough in any case —all but impossible. Assuredly one of Ruskin's masked words is that word "own."

Britain, we are told about ten thousand times a year—particularly of course by German propaganda—owns a quarter of the earth. Again and again it is pointed out that forty-five million people own that quarter, while hundreds of millions in Have-not nations go hungry. We are presented a picture of John Bull as a bloated landowner drawing tributes from the tenants of his vast estates while starvelings outside clamor for the food and raw materials which he refuses to sell, to which he "forbids access" (although it is never clear how he could turn the "vast estates" to profitable account and derive revenues from them unless he did dispose of the products). The plain implication of it all is that there must be "a redistribution of property," if the world is to have peace.

If the reader is disposed to suggest that the writer is himself indulging in fantasy; that no one takes such a word as "owning" in this context as indicating what it usually means—then all one can say is that a vast amount of the literature of this subject has strangely escaped the reader's notice. In a number of previous books, some of them (alas) dating back nearly forty years, the present author has quoted page after page from contemporary political literature, sometimes from the writings of those who bear justly honored names, in which this picture of Britain "owning" a quarter of the world is accepted without question at its face value, as indicating just what the word normally means. Nor does this literature belong merely to the past. It would be possible to cite from books and articles of the last four or five years, numberless passages in which that "ownership" of a "quarter of the earth" figures with all the implications just indicated. It comes often from sources now entirely friendly to the Allied cause, and very often in casual references like that in which Mr. Louis Bromfield, in an article in a recent issue of a popular magazine, remarks that for "every pound Britain has put into India, the British have taken out half a million."

Some years previously an American judge had written:

> The tentacles of England extend everywhere from Halifax to Jamaica, from London to Cape Town, from Gibraltar to Siam; and those tentacles have a sensitive power of suction. . . .
>
> From India, from Australia, from South Africa and from Canada her sons return laden with the profits of newly developed regions. Proprietorship of those regions is thus bringing back its gains. . . .[1]

A brilliant foreign correspondent who has done yeoman's service to the cause of the United Nations, explains, at the time of Mussolini's thrust into Africa, the Fascist aggression in these terms:

> It seems to me there is just as grave a responsibility on the shoulders of the British Government which possesses in the world more than it ever needs to have, which has taken mandates over Palestine and Iraq out of the last war as booty and a good big part of the German colonies in East Africa, and to this day has never offered to give up even 10,000 square miles to satiate either Germany or Italy in order to prevent the next war.
>
> Would you say that Germany and Italy were only the ones to blame? I would say that the "haves" have just as great a responsibility as the "have-nots" for leading the whole world into this terrible thing. Until they are willing to give up something, what chance have we for peace? . . .

---

[1] From *Facing Europe*, by Judge Bausman.

The nations who are the "haves" have to make up their minds to contribute something, and if France and Britain and the other nations who have the chips are not willing to play the chips, they must take part of the moral responsibility before history some day . . .[2]

One of the publications (date 1935) of the American Foreign Policy Association, which exists to put the facts of the international situation before the American public, explaining a chart showing the difference in possessions between the Haves and the Have-nots, says:

The war to end war failed to solve the economic problems that had been its root cause. For back of national jealousies and desire for power is always the pressure for more territory, greater resources, increasing world markets. The chart shows the population of the leading nations, and how much wheat, potatoes, coal, steel, oil and cotton they produced in 1933. . . .

The chart shows why England has built up a great empire of colonies from whom she can import the things she lacks and to whom she can send surplus population and production. . . .

A book entitled *The Price of Peace* (dated 1934), by Mr. Brooks Emery in conjunction with Mr. F. Simonds, explains its purpose thus:

It undertakes to prove that precisely as a century ago European peace was impermanent because of political inequalities existing between the nationalities of the Continent, so to-day world peace is similarly precarious because of the economic disparities existing between nations. . . .

And concludes that:

The world will presently be condemned to witness new struggles between the great powers, some seeking to acquire, others to retain, those resources in raw materials and minerals essential to modern industrial life . . . Patently this price of peace must be paid by those nations, of which the United States is the most striking example, whose material resources bestow the largest measure of economic self-sufficiency.

---

[2] From an address by Leland Stowe before the Executives' Club of Chicago, Friday, October 18th, 1935.

Such quotations could be made indefinitely. The importance of these misconceptions is not merely that they tend to embitter relations between the American and British peoples; that they put British policies and British responsibilities for the world's unrest in a distorting light, but that they turn the public mind in the direction of impracticable or impossible solutions and turn it away from the indispensable solutions. Such conceptions add to heat but not to light. This picture of John Bull as a bloated landowner battening on the miseries of landless people feeds the sense of unfairness, of injustice, of inequity; it produces a scapegoat, inflames indignation. But in fact it furnishes no cure. It does not imply any proposal to abolish imperialism but to redistribute it. It does not propose to reform or abolish economic nationalism but to intensify it, by starting on the assumption that nations are entitled to be, and can be, self-sufficient; should have under their political control the resources necessary for their economic life.

The cure for imperialism is not to increase the number of imperialist states—to increase, that is, the number of vested interests buttressing imperialism—but to transform imperialism into something more just and more workable. But by accepting the idea of Haves and Have-nots we are in danger of making that solution impossible. If it be true that Italians must have colonies or starve, then they have a right to conquer Abyssinia, especially as the Abyssinians would certainly be the better off under Italian rule than under their own. From the moment that we admit that colonies are "a vital need" as a source of raw material and outlets for population we begin to travel, not in the direction of internationalism, but away therefrom. We propose to "do justice" by the perpetuation of an essentially vicious and unjust system. By admitting the claims of an Italy or a Germany to self-sufficiency we imply that we should seek, not to abolish economic nationalism, but to make it workable; we imply that it can be made workable—in a world of some sixty independent sovereign states. (For, of course, if solution is to be along the lines of national self-sufficiency we cannot possibly in equity resist the claims of such Have-not states as Switzerland, Sweden, Norway,

Czechoslovakia, Poland, half-a-dozen Eastern and Central European states, to say nothing of such densely populated territories as parts of India.) The tendency to accept as well-founded the character of the Italian and German claims, means setting out upon a road which can only lead us all farther into the morass.

What Does "Owning" the Empire Mean?

Let us test some of the "masked words" of the quotations a page or two back by comparing them with the facts.

The fact is that Britain does not "own" this Empire at all. She governs a rapidly diminishing area of it. But to fail to make a distinction between "owning" and "governing" is to be guilty of one of those elementary confusions that help to produce those political failures of co-operation which have made the world the victim of totalitarian aggression.

The people of Britain no more "own" their "Empire"—the land, the farms, mines, factories, houses and other properties of Britain's "overseas possessions"—than they "own" the United States, or South America. If an Englishman wants to buy a Canadian house or farm, or a quantity of Canadian wheat or Australian wool he has to pay for it, like any German or Italian, or American. As a matter of simple statistical, financial fact, Americans own, in the proper sense of the term, have title, that is, to far more of mining and railway stock, factories, and hotels and houses, in Canada, a British "possession," than do British citizens. British investments in Canada do not today amount to 15 per cent of the non-Canadian money employed in the country. British citizens own, or have recently owned, in any proper sense of the term, far more property outside their Empire than within: British investments in American countries alone exceed British investments in the whole of the dependent Empire. During a large part of the nineteenth century Britain spent more money in building up the United States (and so, presumably, creating the basis of "tribute"), particularly its railways, than she did upon her own Empire.

Perhaps the facts—or rather the dominant and pertinent fact, the one which matters most—could be brought home by this sweeping but broadly true statement:

If the United States were to annex the whole of the British Empire, lock, stock, and barrel, to become its "owner," to possess all its "vast estate," a "quarter of the earth," the mass of Englishmen (which would include the "capitalists" as well as the workers) would not lose a pound, nor the mass of Americans (which would include the denizens of Wall Street as well as of the East Side) gain a dollar, as the result of this vast "real estate" transaction.

What we so persistently overlook in considering these annexations is that the "annexer" does not merely annex the property, he annexes also the owners of it, who in practice remain the same after annexation as before; not merely does he take over the tax-levying power, but the fulfillment of the services upon which the taxes are expended. Of course, if Hitler managed to re-establish chattel slavery, the thing might be different; the people themselves would be "property." But he has not yet proved that he can permamently enrich even the "master race" by that process, if only because we the "slave races" may have something to say about it. The German people will not be better but worse off, than if the slavery experiment had never been tried.

In the event of the annexation of the British Empire by the United States (or the merging of the two, which would come to the same thing, and which very many in Britain, probably a majority, desire) it is likely that the prosperity of all the peoples of the Empire and the Union would be on sounder foundations; whatever special interests on either side might lose would be counterbalanced by the gain on both sides of other interests. But looking at the people of Britain as one entity, or "owner," and the people of America as another, the first would not lose property, nor the latter gain it, by the "transfer." Indeed, in view of the discussion of such projects as Union Now at present going on, it is probably quite safe to say this: If Britain were formally to make this offer of Union—as Churchill made the offer of immediate union to France in her hour of agony—

there would be great sections in the United States that would refuse the offer of these "possessions" and properties on the precise ground that there was nothing in it for this country. These arguments—that America would carry burdens but little profit in taking over Britain and the Empire—are already part of the Union Now discussion. Quite obviously and undeniably the British do not "own" the Empire in the commonly accepted sense of that term at all.

But since that fact is obvious on a moment's thought, what meaning do those who use such a word attach to it?

The idea seems to be that the political power exercised by Britain enables that country in some way to exact tribute from the Empire—in a way that would not be possible if it were not "Empire," exact it by force, by the power of the British Navy; to "exploit" it economically only because London exercises this political power, and that if that power ceased and the Empire came to an end, economic oppression or exploitation would cease.

Again let us look at the facts. In what way and to what extent does Britain exercise political control over the Empire at all?

The Facts No One Knows

There is a part of this question which, fortunately, is not in the region of opinion, or interpretation at all; but of plain statutory fact; as much in the region of fact as would be the statement that Mayor La Guardia is not appointed by the Emperor of Abyssinia. If one were to make this statement that the mayor's appointment is not made in that way, it would not be doubted very widely; and moderately well-informed people would say that it came as near to objective truth as language when employed about political things can reasonably be expected to come.

But when to audiences anywhere outside the Empire—and to a good many within the Empire—the statement is made that the British government does not govern in Canada or Australia, or New Zealand or Eire or South Africa; that these territories are governed by their own independent governments which can and do erect heavy tariffs against Great Britain; adopt in some cases exclusion laws against British subjects every bit as severe as those adopted by the United States against the same type of immigrant; that Britain has no power of veto over such laws; no powers of taxation; that if a Dominion like Canada comes into the war it is by the free vote of its parliament over which Britain can exercise no compulsion; that if an Eire decides to stay out and to refuse Britain (or America) the use of naval bases, well, that is the end of it, however many British lives and ships it may cost; that, in other words, over much of its area the British Empire has come to an end and been resolved into a group of independent states; that the independence for which the thirteen colonies had to fight has been granted to the Dominions without fighting; that the Statute of Westminster, which registers formally the status of the Dominions is a Declaration of Independence freely accorded—when one makes these statements of fact, well, the auditors or readers in four cases out of five do not believe a word of it.[8] There is a catch in it somewhere; the British know how to get round it; they exercise financial pressure; they exercise social pressure. Anyhow, it is not true. Words and symbols, and familiar pictures of the past, carry far more weight than actual laws or statutes duly written down in the books. Is not Britain an Empire? Empires don't behave that way. What about the king? Cannot he veto any bill of the Canadian or Australian Parliament? The rulers of Britain are imperialists, and imperialists would not

---

[8] The text of the clause in the Statute of Westminster defining the position of the Dominions reads:
No law hereafter made by the Parliament of the United Kingdom shall extend to any of the Dominions as part of the law of that Dominion. . . . No law, and no provision of any law, made after the commencement of this Act by the Parliament of a Dominion shall be void or inoperative on the ground that it is repugnant to the law of England, or to the provisions of any existing or future act of Parliament, of the United Kingdom, or to any order, rule or regulation made under any such act, and the powers of the parliament of a Dominion shall include the power to repeal or amend any such act, order, rule or regulation insofar as the same is part of the law of the Dominion.

have agreed to all that; agreed to the independence of one great territory after another; the passage out of their hands of power over such vast regions of the earth. The thing is absurd; and so, not true.

It has been this writer's habit for many years now to act as director of certain summer seminars of university students of various nationalities, gathered, before this war, in some European capital. Sometimes as many as twenty nationalities have been represented in a gathering of fifty or sixty university students, come together to study the international problem for a month or two.

Here were young men and women from all over the world having enjoyed exceptional educational opportunities; having an especial interest in international affairs; having made a special study of them. The position of the British Empire, the real facts of its nature and composition, any tendencies that it might be revealing, these surely were facts of prime importance in the world. Yet in case after case, a mere cold statement of the statutory facts was met with blank incredulity—and, it must be added, with some resentment, since these facts added a complication to their usually oversimplified theories of economic imperialism. I have known a debate as to whether, in fact, Britain could and did veto Canadian Legislation, go on among these students—inconclusively—day after day. Even when Canadian students were present, patiently insisting that really and truly the Canadian Parliament was supreme, the foreign students would show immense ingenuity in "proving" that the statutes did not state the facts.

Such an attitude is not confined to students. Mr. Theodore Dreiser, in a book of the year of grace 1940, supports them thus:

> Canada . . . has no legal right to keep out of one of England's wars, but automatically becomes a belligerent; it had already been put into the present war by the English Governor-General days before the Parliament "declared war." [4]

Similarly, it would seem with Australia:

---

[4] *America Is Worth Saving*, pp. 112–113.

The golden chains binding Australia to Mother England are so strong that as soon as Holy War was declared last year—and this was done without consulting the Australian Parliament—the removal of all civil liberties along the lines laid down by Mother was energetically proceeded with. The Governor-General, who is sent out from England C.O.D., now has almost complete dictatorial powers, being free to demand information from anyone on any subject on pain of jail, to enter and search premises at will or whim, to arrest without warrant people who "an officer suspects are about to commit an offence." [5]

One would have supposed that Eire, with its refusal of bases, its maintenance of diplomatic relations with Germany, the presence of Germans moving freely about Southern Ireland—that all this would have proof of some fairly large measure of independence under Dominion Status. Not for Mr. Dreiser, who remarks:

The story of Eire, today one of the five "Dominions," is final proof of the fact that England is not and has never been willing, as it claims to be, to grant independent government "when they are ready for it" to Empire peoples other than those of English origin.[6]

But perhaps one of the most striking examples of the domination of the fact by the word, the symbol, the familiar picture, is revealed by a paragraph which recently appeared in Mr. William Randolph Hearst's daily column. In that paragraph Mr. Hearst remarked that we could be pretty sure that Britain would never give up the gold lands of South Africa. Now all power over those lands was surrendered by the British government to the government of the South African Union something over thirty years ago. (Mr. Hearst's column carries the heading "In the News.") The government of the South African Union, headed at present by a Boer general who led armies against Britain in the Boer War, has just as much power over those gold lands as the government of Mr. DeValera has over the naval bases of Southern Ireland; and the British government has no more power over those gold lands than it has over the Irish

[5] *Ibid.*, pp. 112–113.
[6] Ibid., p. 111.

naval bases; no more power in fact over the mines of the Transvaal than it has over those of Colorado or California. Oh! but, immediately objects the skeptic, the shares in the South African mines are held largely by London financiers. Well, there was a time when a good many shares in the California and Colorado mines were held in London; when majority holdings in some cases (as also in early American oil and railway enterprises) were British. It did not make those states part of the British Empire, did not deprive them, or the United States generally, of their political independence. And though some political importance was attached by Americans to the independence (to state the case mildly), it could and did coexist with a large use of British capital, just as today Canada so largely uses American capital. Incidentally, if the independent government of the South African Union decided to tax, or confiscate, the property of the British shareholders in the gold fields or the diamond fields, with the kind of ruthlessness that Eire has adopted in the confiscation of certain forms of British property in Ireland, it is as certain as anything can be in politics that the British government would be even more helpless to prevent it than it was in the case of the Irish properties. All of which does not prevent Mr. Hearst saying with complete and unchallenged assurance, that "Britain will never give up the gold lands of the Transvaal."

There is something in his paragraph still more suggestive. To the statement that "England never abandons anything—never any commercial benefit, never any military advantage, never valuable territory" he adds also this: "never any strategic harbor." Now, in the very issue of the paper in which this paragraph appears, was a dispatch from Dublin indicating that Mr. De Valera was standing as adamantly as ever in his refusal of the use of the naval bases by Britain. But less than three years previously those bases had been in British occupation (having been reserved in the original Anglo-Irish Treaty of 1922 and evacuated in 1938 voluntarily as a gesture of good will to the Irish, and with a view to improving the temper of Anglo-Irish relations, to removing an Irish grievance). It is possible that Mr. Hearst was genuinely unaware of the setting up of an independent Union government in Africa over thirty years ago. But he could hardly have been ignorant of the fact that Britain did not occupy the Irish bases at the time he wrote, and did occupy them a few years previously. This obvious fact, however, is as nothing in the face of the power of words used during a lifetime: the words being "empire" and "imperialism"; connoting, as another journalist put it, "booty, loot"; and looters do not ever give up things. Therefore no strategic harbor has been given up—even when it has.

To ignore, however, the de-imperialization of the British Empire which has gone on is to ignore one of the most significant tendencies, and some of the most significant facts of modern history.

Here are half-a-dozen nations that have achieved their independence, not by war, but as the result of friendly discussion with the imperial power. These new nations contain a population many times larger than was the population of the thirteen colonies which had to fight for the same independence.

This event—that the freedom for which in the eighteenth century peoples had to fight is now granted without fighting—has passed, all but completely unnoticed. So far as the "big public" is concerned, they have never even heard of it, as we have just seen. One of the great occurrences of modern history has gone unrecorded in the popular press of the world. And it went unrecorded just because it was a peaceful achievement. If there had been wars of liberation the story would have resounded throughout the world. Because it took place in peace, the persistence of the masked words and the ancient symbols have caused it to pass unnoticed. Yet the fact that the change was achieved peacefully did not make it less significant, it made it more so.

A German Liberal, an economist, an ex-member of the Reichstag, and a German enemy of Hitler, now an American citizen, has commented on that strange fact in these terms:

> This emergence of totally independent nations within the tenuous yet tenacious frame of the British Empire, with all its deep implications, was, curiously enough, overlooked everywhere outside the Empire. The world heard without much interest the unfamiliar words

of that new term for the old empire, a "British Commonwealth of Nations." It noted in passing that in 1931 such an unusual thing for Britain as a written constitution was enacted for this Commonwealth in the Statute of Westminster. How many in the United States took the trouble to study the potentialities of this departure? Who popularized it among the citizens of the world as a creative idea for a less chaotic future relationship among independent yet united nations? Who glorified this feat of British political genius and imagination, achieved even in that tired first decade after Versailles? Unheeded the age-old and ever-new British concepts of "Imperium et Libertas," of liberty through unity, of freedom under self-imposed law, made their entry into international affairs in our time.

Inside this British Commonwealth of Nations, which well-known writers still flippantly treat as the domain of British capitalist "imperialism," there are in Australia's and New Zealand's Labor regimes those laboratories of social experiments and planned economy ventures. There is, in Canada, that laboratory for minority rights of one of the great old Western nations and religions against a majority of another—French Catholics against English Protestants—in which relationship Britain still functions behind the scene as the minority guardian. There is South Africa, that laboratory of racial politics in which the more progressive and daringly liberal native policies in the old British colonies, the Cape Colony and Natal, have to find some common ground with the much narrower racial concepts of the Boer and German elements in the Transvaal and the Orange Free State (originally settled in protest against Britain's abolition of slavery); not to forget the problems of Indian indentured labor and Indian civil rights in South Africa that have been solved equitably thanks to the efforts of young Gandhi and his British supporters—January 1, 1920, is India's "Abolition Day." And there is that laboratory of world trade relations among agricultural and monocultural, old industrial and young industrial, countries that all went for direction and satisfaction to the Ottawa Imperial Economic Conference of 1932. In every instance, the influence of the mother country was in the line of liberalism, moderation, trusteeship for minority rights, creative compromise, and—unceasing self-criticism.[7]

---

[7] Gustave Stolper: *This Age of Fable* (pp. 246–247), Reynal and Hitchcock, New York.

While considering the tyranny of words we would do well to ask just precisely what we mean by "economic imperialism." Was it economic imperialism for Englishmen to lend Americans money wherewith to build the early railroads or open up the early mines? Is it imperialism for Englishmen to build railroads in Brazil? Or in the Argentine? Ought countries like Brazil or the Argentine—lacking industrial development, lacking capital—to have waited until they could build the railroads themselves opening up their undeveloped countries so very, very slowly? It would not have made for the raising of the standard of life either in those South American countries, or in Britain. The economic fact underlying the elaborate financial arrangements of the thing—even when those financial arrangements were not always very savory—was this: "The British in effect said to the South Americans: We will build the railroads, and that will help you develop your country, and with its products, beet, corn, hides, you will pay us later." For years now the workers of Birmingham and Manchester have eaten cheap Argentinian beef because their fathers built the railroads or established the refrigerating plants or what not, while the Brazilians and Argentinians are, on their side, living in better houses, at a higher standard of life because of their English-built railroads or other industrial developments.

Is there anything very antisocial or immoral in this process of itself? You may get graft or corruption when a city raises loans to build a reservoir or install a sewage system. But after all the graft is incidental. If reservoirs were never built nor sewage systems created because there might be graft in the financial arrangements, the world quite obviously would be the poorer; and the sicker.

But to judge by the tone of much writing on "economic imperialism" the very operation of an old country using its resources to develop a new one is in itself evil.

When Mr. Louis Bromfield tells us that "for every pound invested in India British capitalists have taken over 500,000 pounds," [8] one wonders just what precise meaning the statement carried to his

---

[8] *Liberty Magazine*, May 16, 1942.

mind. The great capital investments in India have been in the rail-roads and the irrigation system—the latter by far the greatest in the world. India's two great needs, since the ancient scourge of the country has been famine, were railroads and irrigation. The build-ing of 40,000 miles of railroads has enormously diminished the famine risk owing to the more effective distribution of grain and agricultural products. The irrigation system has no parallel any-where. Over twenty thousand miles of canals are operated in the Punjab alone and over fourteen million acres are irrigated under the system. Under one single project—that of the Bhakra Dam which will be 394 feet high—the area to be irrigated will be four times the whole irrigated area of Egypt.

It is these projects which have absorbed a large part of the capital invested in India. When Mr. Bromfield tells us he believes the state-ment that the British have taken from such enterprises half a mil-lion for every pound invested, does he mean that exorbitant in-terest rates have been charged upon the capital? Because in that case the statement is quite capable of precise and exact investigation. The accounts of these great enterprises are published and have for years been subject to every form of scrutiny. About finance in India two generalizations can be made: If India had had to depend solely upon her native moneylenders the capital she employed would have been among the costliest in the world; under the system of British guaranteed loans she has had some of the cheapest. If the building of those 40,000 miles of railroad had depended upon Indian capital, we can say, with fair assurance, judging from the experience of China, that most of them would never have been built at all.

Indeed, Mr. John Gunther—notwithstanding a decisively anti-imperialist slant—reflects in his book *Inside Asia* that if only China had "possessed a system of communications like that of India, the history of China in recent years would have been very different, though one might also say that if China had it, China would not have been China, but a British preserve." [9] Of which one critic of

---

[9] Note a further comparison between India and China. In a dispatch from India at the very height of the recent disturbances (September 12, 1942)

Mr. Gunther's book remarks that this would seem to imply that it is better to stick to famine, floods, internal wars, defenselessness from foreign aggressors, rather than seek the aid of foreign capital or foreign power. Yet every one of the United Nations has to face the fact today that its defense depends in part upon foreign power, that it cannot stand alone. And most nations have used foreign capital. America herself did not hesitate to use British capital in the construction of her early railroads; and Monroe and Jefferson (as they so freely acknowledged) were glad to "marry themselves to the British navy" for aid in defense against invasion.[10]

Examine for just a moment this charge that for every dollar invested by the British in India they have withdrawn half a million. The sterling debt of India—the largest item in what is commonly called the "drain" of wealth from India—is part of a financial structure which has enabled that debt to be very rapidly reduced, and the interest charges to be so lowered that today an average of about 4.5 per cent interest has been reduced to 3.5 per cent, a rate far below the best credit conditions ever enjoyed by independent Asiatic

---

Mr. Edgar Snow, the distinguished American correspondent, cables: "In many ways the Indians are freer than we are at home now. To a great extent they enjoy freedom of organisation, freedom of the press and freedom of assembly. They have infinitely more, all of them, under the British government than the Chinese possess in Free China. They speak their minds with absolute freedom. No Gestapo menaces the personal security of their homes . . . I have seen Communist mass meetings and demonstrations in the streets of Calcutta, Delhi, and Bombay where the crowds shouted the slogans of world revolution and denounced British imperialism. Red flags flew untrammeled in the breeze . . . At Wardha, all through the meeting where Gandhi and the Congress plotted to oust the British Raj, there was no attempt to break up the gathering nor even any policeman in the vicinity. *Harijan*, published in many languages, and apparently without censorship, carried the threat of rebellion over the country."

[10] Mr. Raymond Leslie Buell, in his survey of "Relations with Britain" published by *Fortune Magazine*, notes of the early years of the nineteenth century: "During this period America's economic development, north and south of the Rio Grande, was largely a part of British economic expansion. American railways were built with British money; immigrants came to American shores in British vessels, across an ocean patrolled by the British Navy. Our industries made use of mechanical equipment produced in the British Isles. American agriculture, particularly cotton and wheat, depended upon the British market. American statesmen grasped the fact that British sea power stood between the United States and the expansionist monarchies of the continent."

states such as China or Japan. Furthermore, this sterling debt is invested in self-supporting enterprises—railroads, canals, and the like—so that there is hardly any drain on the Indian general tax payer. The railroads are for the most part government-owned, so that the British rule in India has resulted in a bit of "Socialism" for which American Socialists are still clamoring in the United States; but with so far no notable success. Indeed a recent examination of the statistics involved reveals the striking fact that the interest charge on the entire public debt of India in the widest sense is actually more than covered by the income from assets created with the help of that debt.

In particular, the state-owned railways of India, with their muster-roll of more than 600,000 employees, constitute one of the largest business enterprises in the world, with a capital of $2,196,000,000 and the money which has been raised for this purpose may reasonably be regarded as in effect the capital of a great business rather than as national debt in the ordinary sense.

Moreover, to an extent that is rarely realized, Indian and British finance have become disentangled. The Financial Editor of the Manchester *Guardian* recently [11] pointed out that by the end of the current year the last of the great India stock will be repaid and British capital investments in India will be reduced to very modest commercial proportions.

As late as March, 1936, the Indian government's sterling debt was the equivalent of $1,504,000,000. After repayment of the 3.5 per cent stock in January, 1942, there was only about $388,000,000 of the sterling debt left; much of it will probably be held outside Britain. He adds:

> No loan has been raised by the Indian government in London since 1912. With growing internal capital resources and the improvement in financial facilities, it became possible to raise all the money needed from Indian investors. At the same time it became an official policy to reduce the sterling debt or convert it to lower interest rates.
> In the last three or four years, an enormous amount of debt has

---

[11] July, 1942.

been repatriated by the cancellation of sterling loans and their replacement by rupee loans. . . .

But all this is only the negative side of the process. The positive side is that Indian nationals have been taking over the ownership of immensely valuable productive enterprises which have been created by fifty years of indebtedness to British investors. Almost the whole of the public debt of India has been incurred for developing productive enterprises. This has had almost the incredible result that India has today virtually no national debt in the accepted sense.

In the article in which he expresses the view that Britain has taken out half a million dollars for every dollar invested, Mr. Bromfield declares that the British capitalist and merchant banker class and the Indian civil servant class were responsible for a policy in India which had but one purpose: "the exploitation of India as a market for British-manufactured products and as a reservoir of raw materials to supply British factories and load British ships."

But he also notes that of late years India has become increasingly self-sufficient industrially, particularly in cotton and steel. What he fails to point out is that this result is due in no small measure to a fact which seems to be all but completely unknown abroad, namely, that for over twenty years India has enjoyed the right to make her own tariff, a right which she has exercised to the very great detriment of British interests. The protective policy which India has adopted for the exclusion of British goods has, as this writer who sat for some years in the British House of Commons for a textile city has very good reason to know, brought widespread injury and suffering to industries in Lancashire and Yorkshire. Yet, this suffering of British populations was accepted by Britain as a necessary result of the freedom which had been granted India to make her own tariff, (under the Fiscal Autonomy Convention of 1921) and with which the British interests concerned were not allowed to interfere. If the picture so widely current of a Britain financially oppressing India had any validity, here surely was an occasion on which the imperial power would be exercised in order to come to the rescue of the stricken industry of Lancashire. It was not exercised despite some

Indian charges to the contrary. George Schuster, who knows the economic problems of India as few living Europeans do, writes:

> Any idea that Britain can use her political position to impose on India commercial policies to British advantage has been absolutely abandoned. In recent years, with India, just as with the self-governing Dominions, the political ties of the Commonwealth have afforded an opportunity for discussing reciprocal trade arrangements of mutual advantage. But these arrangements have been freely concluded as between equals, and the trade figures indicate that it is India, in finding British markets for her products—rather than vice versa—that has benefited from the sentimental and political ties that exist between the two countries.[12]

One very common criticism is that a "vast British bureaucracy" battens on the Indian tax payer. As to that the reader can, if he will, go through an interesting experience. Let him ask any ordinarily well-educated friend how many British officials there are likely to be in a country of nearly four hundred million people, possessing great state enterprises like the railroads. Remind him that the numbers of those in government employ in a country like America—with hardly more than a third of India's population—run, when federal, state, city, and county governments are taken into account, into several million persons. What, on that basis, the reader might ask a few friends, would be a fair number of British officials in India? If the reader's experience in any way resembles mine he will get guesses ranging all the way from ten thousand to half a million.

---

[12] *India and Democracy.* The Macmillan Company, London, 1941.

The trade figures demonstrate Schuster's contention. In the five years up to 1914 India imported as an annual average from the United Kingdom goods worth £61 millions and exported to the United Kingdom goods worth £37½ millions, i. e., a favorable U. K. balance of £23½ millions. In the last full year before the present war, 1938–9, the position had been completely reversed. Indian imports from the United Kingdom were £34.8 millions and her exports to the U. K. £43½ millions, i. e., a favorable Indian balance of £8½ millions. In the pre-1914 period India took 63 per cent of her imports from the U. K. and sent to the U. K. 25 per cent of her exports. In 1938–9 imports from the U. K. were no more than 30½ per cent of India's imports while the proportion of India's exports which went to the U. K. had risen to 34½ per cent.

There are not half a million; there are not ten thousand. The Indian Civil Service contains—or contained just before the war—under six hundred Englishmen. Does it look as though India had been used as a means of finding fat jobs for Englishmen? Is it quite decent to talk of "vast hordes of British officials battening on an impoverished people" as this writer has heard a critic do?

The fact that there are only a few hundred British in the Civil Service of this vast continent means that its administration is in native hands and has not been kept in the hands of the British: that India is, administratively, governing herself. There have, of late, been many and bitter criticisms of British administration in the East. Yet more than one outside observer, facing the strange fact of the British element in the Indian administration being limited to any such number as five hundred men, has described the thing as administrative magic.

The Dangers of Misinformation

We are dealing here perhaps rather with a misapprehension as to the actual facts, than with confusion as to the use of terms, but the facts themselves are important in this connection because they bear upon our view as to the line of solution. The remedy which the nations apply for the solution or alleviation of the very real economic difficulties which face them, will depend upon the extent to which they are dominated by, or are free from, these elementary confusions. If the possessive presumptions dominate; if it is thought to be true, as a very distinguished journalist wrote a year or two since, that "it is a matter of life and death for Germany and Italy and Japan to break the blockade which is throttling the economic activities of both"; if it be true, as he goes on to say, "that the situation is made the more intolerable for the hungry because those who are fed today owe their good fortune to the fact that they were bad yesterday"— if that sort of view dominates the public mind, then we shall probably see the attempt made at solution along the lines of territorial redistribution, and that means more and more of economic nationalism and less and less of economic internationalism, by which alone we can be saved.

Yet the facts which discredit the notion that a nation's prosperity depends upon the extent of its colonies or conquered territory would seem to be obvious enough.

If in fact a nation added to the property of its people every time it annexed territory, we should find the people of the Great Empires rich and those of the little countries poor. But it does not work out that way. The people of Have-not states like Switzerland, Sweden, Denmark, Norway, with no colonies, no Empire, had a general standard of life just as high as—in many respects higher than—the standard of the people of great Empire-possessing countries like Britain and France.

The idea that a country must produce within its frontiers the raw materials necessary for its industries has no support in fact or history. Britain's greatest export trade—Lancashire cotton products—was based upon the raw material of a foreign state, America. Britain did not have to conquer Georgia or Louisiana to get the raw materials in question.

There are something like fifty independent states in the world—many of them less self-sufficient than the three great totalitarian countries. If we are to solve world friction by giving to each what it needs, are we going to give Switzerland an outlet to the sea and Sweden rubber plantations? And if we could make them self-sufficient today, they would not be tomorrow. Forty years ago we should all have clamored for coal and not worried about rubber or oil. Today it is the latter we should most insist upon.

The quantitative unimportance of colonies is equally ignored. Before the war Germany drew exactly 0.5 per cent of the raw material she used from her colonies. She could still have drawn that amount even if they had not been colonies. She drew as much therefrom after Versailles. More Germans were earning their livelihood in the city of Paris in July, 1914, than in all the German colonies of the world combined.

It will be said: If colonies are as valueless as all that why does Britain keep them?

The reply to which is: First, she is not keeping them. Most of her Empire (Canada, Australia, South Africa) has already become independent; India and much of the rest is on the way thereto. Secondly, while government of the colonies may bring no very great advantage to Britain, government by others would probably bring her considerable disadvantages and danger.

Which brings us to the question at issue.

The real difficulties from which Germany and other totalitarian states suffered was not that raw materials were not within their borders (for the producer of raw materials anywhere, everywhere, wants to sell them), but that in order to get the raw materials the German, or the Italian, had to pay for them, and to get the money to pay for them he had to sell his own goods. And that was made difficult by rising tariffs, preferences, exclusions, quotas, exchange restrictions— every device of a fanatical economic nationalism.

It was not mainly a colonial question at all. Less than 5 per cent of the world's raw materials are produced in colonies, less than that proportion of the world's trade is done with colonies. Denmark suffered immeasurably more by Britain's adoption of a protective tariff than Germany did by the "loss" of her colonies. Germany and Italy suffered more by the Ottawa preferences and the raising of the American tariff than by their lack of colonial territory.

But the totalitarian countries did not want an internationalist solution at all. They wanted to be in a position to do the very thing which they blamed Britain for doing: to create ring fences, whether in China or Abyssinia or elsewhere, to keep territories strictly to themselves. Their motive was, of course, largely political and military. In war it *is* a military disadvantage to be dependent either on foreign trade or foreign raw material. Economic self-sufficiency then possesses great military value; and African colonies perhaps may be a source of black man power. Once more we get back to the fact that much of economic nationalism finds its roots in the search for security. We can never create a stable international economy and get over such difficulties as territorial maldistribution may set up, until we have made progress in the problem of general security.

The totalitarian countries will reject offers to share existing empires on equal terms so long as they believe that by threat of war they can become unquestioned masters of much of such territory. They, not unnaturally, prefer complete "ownership" to mere partnership.

An international order, putting an end to imperialism, cannot be established, obviously, unless the efforts at conquest for the purpose of monopoly position are resisted.

But mere resistance on the part of the democracies, if it is for the purpose of maintaining the right to do as they please with colonies —which the dictators also desire to do—would place the contestants on the same moral plane. The democracies must have a better case morally than the dictators.

The democracies must make it plain that they stand for the defense of their countries and empires, not for the purpose of maintaining the right to close them against the world, but for the purpose of ensuring that they are not conquered and then closed against themselves, and made the basis of attack against themselves. They must make it plain that they really do offer *partnership*, partnership not alone in the economic advantages, but partnership also in the power by which the law that will defend all alike shall be maintained.

But, again, that offer will not be accepted if the totalitarian states are in a position to say: "Why should we accept partnership when we are in a position to secure possession and domination?"

We must show that that resistance, and the unity and co-operation by which alone it can be made effective, has become not merely a wartime feature of the life of democracies, but part of their peacetime life as well.

The right alternative to imperialism is not anarchy, which would deliver the world to Hitler, but a Society of Nations. This is extremely difficult to organize and will be impossible if we insist on tearing to pieces such political integrations as the centuries have produced and starting de novo on the basis of nineteenth-century nationalist "independence" and self-determination. If some anti-imperialist advice had been taken Hitler would by now have won the war. The cases of India, Ireland, Panama, Iceland, Greenland, as illustrating alternatives and dilemmas.

CHAPTER VIII

The Alternatives

WE HAVE seen that the major motives behind the two World Wars are to be found where we should expect to find deep motives—in the instinct of self-preservation, defense. In a world where a nation has nothing to depend upon but its own individual power for the defense of its most vital rights, it attempts to be stronger than any who might challenge those rights. But what in that case, of the defense of the weaker? Is he to go without defense? The scramble for preponderance means that the security of one involves the insecurity of some other.

Nations have attempted to find a solution in a "balance" of power. But no one can really say when two nations or groups are equal in power. And a balance can be upset overnight by a new alliance (as Russia upset the relative European balance when she abandoned the Western nations and made her compact with Germany a few weeks before the outbreak of the present war).

The internal organization of our nations indicates how power may be used for the maintenance of peace. Instead of each party in the state—Democrats, Republicans, what not—attempting to possess more physical power than a rival, all agree to stand behind the constitution which will use the power of the community to see that no one is the victim of violence.

Unless we can somehow manage to apply this principle—*"all against the aggressor"*—to the international field we shall either continue to get what we have been getting (recurrent wars becoming more and more devastating), or the conquest of all by one who will impose peace (on his terms) upon those who were unable to create a society by free co-operation. In other words the alternatives are (1) to create voluntarily a free society—organizing collectively its power for the defense of each of its members; or (2) to continue the international anarchy with wars becoming ever more ferocious; or (3) be conquered by one power who will enforce peace and order of a kind.

Freedom and democracy can only develop out of order, law. Where the individual will submit to no rule, there can be no real freedom for anyone. Complete freedom for everybody to drive as he saw fit on the automobile road would give very little freedom indeed. Without a traffic code none could safely use the road. If traffic had fallen into utter chaos the first need would be to establish order; get some rule, good or bad; effectively police the road and impose the code. Afterwards could come the discussion as to the best code; what faults of policing should be corrected.

We see the development of freedom and democracy following broadly that line: first authority and power to impose law; then discussion and criticism by those living under it; then concession of their right to amend or abolish it—and then their right to make it. First, government of the people by authority and power; then, government for the people because authority needs their co-operation; lastly, as that co-operation develops, government by the people. The historians of government and law have a name for the process. They call it development from status to contract. Imperialism has played its part in this process throughout the world. The Roman Empire did give the greater part of the civilized world some two centuries of peace and order. This present writer once heard an American radical and Socialist (a very eminent one indeed), speaking at a meeting where Indians had been voicing their grievances in somewhat violent terms, say this:

When the Roman Empire went to pieces it was followed by the Dark Ages of ignorance, hunger, famine, pestilence, violence, and utter chaos so that men came to look back upon the Empire as a veritable golden age. Will something similar happen in Asia when the British and Dutch Empires go to pieces?

To ask that question is not to defend imperialism. It is to utter the needed warning that it does not suffice merely to smash it; for it is extremely easy to get something still worse. To prevent that result we should recognize that it may be necessary to retain non-democratic authority until democratic authority has been sufficiently developed to take its place.

With all its defects the British Empire has revealed strongly the tendency to transfer power from the imperium to the subject; from an imperial center to the peoples of the Empire. As we have already seen, power at the center has been completely relinquished over the vast areas of Canada, Australia, South Africa, New Zealand. The Act of the imperial Parliament no longer runs in those Dominions. The Empire there has come to an end and has resolved itself into an alliance or league of independent states.

But the Empire was not thus dissolved until co-operation between the parts for mutual defense had been secured by a voluntary tie replacing that of authority. The states of the Commonwealth would all stand together in the event of attack upon any. If the British peoples had been content to say: "Imperialism is undemocratic; repudiate it; smash it; get rid of it; let each colony be completely free"—if that had been the attitude toward the Empire, as something not to be transformed but simply destroyed, the democracies of Britain, Eire, Australia, New Zealand, South Africa would not now exist, for the Nazi power would be master of them all; and would be using them as the means of assault upon the United States. For obviously if in 1939 there had been no "Empire" to help Britain —not merely no Canada, no Australia, no New Zealand, no Africa, but no Gibraltar, no Malta—the British people could not have stood up during the two and a half years of war before America came in.

There has been bitter criticism both in the press and in Congress of Britain's conduct in India. Of that more presently. But if we are to find a decent substitute for imperialism we must face the nature of the forces which have brought it into being, in order that the substitute may prove adequate to meet those forces.

Imperialism of the British type is mainly a by-product of the international anarchy; a desire to retain relative power, and not to see sources of power fall into rival hands in a world where a nation's sole means of defense is its own relative strength.

The motives which have kept Britain in India, for instance, have not been mainly economic. Britain has had of late years as great an economic stake in South America, which she does not control politically, as she has in India. And a free India which was stable and prosperous would not furnish less of commercial "tribute," but probably more, than a resentful India using its tariff-making powers and its boycotts to inflict the maximum damage upon British trade.

The fundamental forces, in other words, which have carried Britain to India are the motives which will keep American forces there, and in Iceland and Egypt and Ireland for the duration. They are political, rooted in the instinct of self-preservation, survival.

In her struggles for survival Britain has been confronted with the alternative which confronts every great state in an anarchic world: to subdue certain other territories or to see them used as an instrument for her own subjugation. It is a struggle which, among other things, has produced the United States.

If Britain, having defeated the Spanish Armada, had not continued to fight Spain in the New World; if Britain had not defeated France in India, it is unlikely that the French would have been defeated in America, and the United States as we know it would not have come into being.

Whether something better or worse would have resulted from British defeat no man can tell. But the only chance of bringing such conflicts to an end is to devise another method of attaining that defense at which they aimed.

Whatever succeeds imperialism must, if it is to be an improvement, avoid a worsening of the kind of anarchy and Balkanization which has already put the democracies of Continental Europe at Hitler's mercy. Yet the alternatives suggested by so many critics of imperialism would in fact expose us all—Asiatic and European alike—to just that risk.

It seems to be almost universally assumed that the whole problem could be solved if only Britain would proclaim the independence of India, or Ireland, or Palestine as the case may be. The issue is taken to be almost purely a moral one, in which, on one side, we have imperial power clinging to ancient privilege, and on the other "peoples rightly struggling to be free."

Thus, as part of a recent discussion of the Irish bases question, a New York weekly publication in its issue of February 7, 1942, has this editorial comment:

> The Irish are painfully aware that England has denied them justice and they are convinced that their age-old enemy has not changed. When England makes restitution for her many conquests, gives back Gibraltar to Spain, Ireland to the Irish, India to the Indians, loosens her grip on Egypt and other territories, it will be time enough to believe that she has turned over a new leaf. Until that time comes, it is futile to talk of trusting a centuries-old aggressor.

That comment is more blunt than most, but it expresses in simple form the assumption which runs through so much of the discussion —that the essence of the Indian, the Irish, and similar imperial problems is a struggle between sheer power and moral right.

The real difficulty, of course, in the Indian problem is that the form of freedom or self-government acceptable to one section in India would be regarded as a gross betrayal of their rights and interests by other sections; and that to proclaim "independence" in merely general terms before some agreement on internal differences had been arrived at, would be to run the risk of repeating in the case of India the present Irish difficulty in a far more serious form.

"There are about fifteen Irelands in the Indian problem," someone remarked the other day.

Separation of Eire from Britain, before resolving the Ulster-Catholic-Protestant problem—an internal conflict within Ireland— has deprived America and the other United Nations of naval bases which were available to America previous to Eire's secession—a loss of power to us and an addition to the enemy's power, which bears most vitally upon that Battle of the Atlantic which we must win if we are not to lose the war, and which at the moment of writing we are so far from winning that the sinking of ships goes on faster than we can build them.

Assume for a moment that Britain had accepted the advice proffered by the anti-imperialist quoted above, and had "turned over a new leaf," not merely to the extent of turning over naval bases to an independent Ireland, but had, as suggested, done an analogous thing in the case of Gibraltar, Malta, Cyprus, Palestine, the Suez Canal region, Aden, the Sudan, Iraq, Iran, the colonies of the East and West African coast (the latter with their harbors so very close to the South American bulge), Malaya, Burma, India, the Pacific Islands on the approach to Australia. Suppose all those places had been granted "complete independence" in the Irish sense, an independence, that is, which is regarded as quite incompatible with any obligation to co-operate with others for mutual defense; each insisting, like Eire, upon the right to be neutral in "Britain's wars" even though Britain be but one among a score, and however defensive the war might be; the right to give hospitality to the agents and diplomats of the enemies of those twenty; as does Eire.

What would have happened to the "liberated" Gibraltars, Egypts, Maltas, Palestines, African and Pacific territories, cut off from all connection with Britain this last twenty years? The reply to that question is to be found in the position of the independent states of the European continent today: they would all be in Axis hands.

The Battle of the Atlantic would have been over long since. For Britain would have been overwhelmed. Her bases, harbors, shipbuilding and factory resources would, like those of France, be in German hands. As Britain is far less self-sufficient than France in the matter of food, German pressure upon the former for "collaboration" could be that much greater.

A helpless government in Britain might be desperately trying to buy better conditions for the British people by concessions to the conqueror in the matter of warships and naval facilities. With the resources of the European continent and of the British Empire in

Europe and Africa having become part of Germany's war resources, and the Battle of the Atlantic having gone in Germany's favor, with the Middle East and India and the command of the Indian Ocean in Axis hands, the Battle of the Pacific would have gone in Japan's favor.

What would have been the outlook for the United States? For the preservation of a free and democratic world? Does anyone, can anyone, deny that at the very least there would have been great likelihood of the result as indicated, if Britain had proceeded on the principle that it is politically immoral to occupy any but her own territory, and that respect for freedom demands that a world-wide system of association be torn to shreds?

It is true that those who demand complete severance of the ties between Britain and such territories as Egypt, or Iraq, or India, argue that if only complete independence of these units be granted and the existing organization be torn completely to pieces, the pieces will by some magic all come together again and work harmoniously for their common defense.

This was the argument used with great eloquence by the supporters of Mr. Chamberlain when in 1938 the naval bases of Southern Ireland (reserved for Britain in the original Anglo-Irish treaty) were turned over to Mr. de Valera's government. The gesture would, we are told, so conciliate the Irish that they would never dream of denying Britain the bases if ever she were in peril.

Mr. de Valera's very Irish argument was, as Mr. Churchill put it at the time, that the only way to unite the two islands was to dissolve every possible connection between them. In the last war, when Ireland was part of the United Kingdom, the American fleet had full use of the bases. Independence deprives America of that use.

But Eire merely illustrates a common experience. When the units of the Austrian Empire, instead of replacing the empire with a workable federalism, simply tore it apart and Balkanized it, the resulting "independent" sections did not agree one with the other. They engaged in bitter feuds over a variety of partitions, and each within itself had minorities ready to claim independence from the newly created government. The final outcome has been German conquest.

The fallacy of the idea that complete independence is the proper alternative to imperialism and will of itself solve the most urgent and agonizing problem that now confronts civilized man—effective protection against the evil violence of an organized criminal minority —is revealed, of course, most strikingly by the plight of the states of Continental Europe now conquered by Hitler. France, the Low Countries, the Scandinavian states, and the other older nations had all been "liberated" from any imperial domination ages since. They were all free peoples, but their freedom could not be defended, however well they fought, because they all refused to create any real union for mutual defense. And that is just why Hitler was so easily able to pick them off one at a time. Because they refused to hang together it was so easy for him to hang them separately.

The other day *The Nation*, which has so often befriended Irish causes, remarked that "the fact that Northern Ireland remains part of the United Kingdom is very probably responsible for Britain's continued existence, for had all Ireland remained neutral, the German blockade might well have succeeded."

The point about that observation is that if, as the result of Irish neutrality, the blockade had succeeded, it is not merely Britain that would have gone under. Ireland would have done so too. The proposition that a powerful nation should commit suicide on behalf of an unfriendly small and weak one may have a sort of lunatic-nationalist logic in it. But if the suicide will mean the end of the smaller nation as well, the whole idea parts company with the world of political reality or explainability.

What Duties Go with Freedom

Yet it is exactly the Eire example which is held up by so many anti-imperialists as the true alternative to imperialism! The whole subject will remain bedeviled by confusion and a fruitful source of disunity among the United Nations, until it ceases to be dominated by two or three absurd fundamental assumptions.

One is that the retention of any ties between Britain and overseas territories is just a manifestation of oppressive imperialism on Britain's part.

Another fallacious assumption is that it is right and moral in a world where integration is so extremely difficult and disintegration so extremely easy, for any member of an old political society to insist not merely that it should get a square deal in the community of states—which it is entitled to do—but that its proper status should be one of "complete freedom"—freedom from all obligations whatsoever to other members of the society, although the world now knows that the price that must be paid for the preservation of freedom is the acceptance of those obligations—sometimes onerous—by which alone it can be defended.

If the story of human association tells us anything, it is that where all demand complete freedom, none has any.

It is a strange fact that so often the progressive who insists we must create a new order which shall be worth the sacrifices of free peoples wants the retention in international politics of conceptions which are very much indeed of the old order and which lie at the root of our present miseries.

The rightness of "absolute" independence and neutrality is one such conception. It involves repudiation of the moral obligation by which alone humane society can be maintained: the obligation of each to do his part in the defense of the victim of lawless violence.

To repudiate that obligation, so that each has to defend himself as best he may, necessarily exposes the great mass of men to domination by a ruthless and violent minority, since the minority can apply to the unorganized mass "the simple and deadly plan of one by one."

In the period of political evolution which confronts us let us talk less of independence, which none can have in any civilized society, and more of equality of right, which all can have; less of neutrality, which would inevitably deliver the majority over to organized violence, and more of partnership in the defense of law, by which alone that Right to Life for which we now fight can be made secure.

American Opinion and the Indian Problem

One supreme consideration at this particular juncture stands out in the three-cornered discussion of the Indian problem. It would be disastrous if a dispute between Indian or Irish parties, or between those parties and the British government, should somehow become a dispute between the American and British peoples or governments.

Such a dispute would hardly serve the interests of the United States, or India, or Ireland, or any member of the United Nations. It would play completely, however, the game of the Axis, which is now turning all its heavy propaganda guns—as anyone who listens to the German radio can judge for himself—to creating division between Britain and America. This propaganda emphasis is presumably based on the fact that, though this country may have more in common with Britain than with any of the other Allies, Britain happens also to be the only one with which America has been twice at war; a fact which has left its mark on American folklore and feeling.

Much weight is attached in Britain to American opinion on the Indian question, just as in the past weight has been given to American opinion on the Irish question, which it may be recalled has sometimes received strong congressional expression. I heard more than one member of the British Parliament a year or two since defend the evacuation of the Irish bases by the Chamberlain government on the ground that it was the kind of thing which would placate Irish-American hostility, and so improve British relations with the United States. They were perhaps not unmindful of the fact that while there has been for so long an Irish vote in America, there has never been an English vote.

The all but unanimous view in America at the time of the British negotiations with Mr. de Valera, who received then much the same moral support that Mr. Nehru receives now, was that no qualification or limitation of any kind ought to be placed upon Ireland's independence. The warnings voiced by Mr. Churchill in opposing Mr. Chamberlain's cession of the bases—warnings so startlingly and tragically vindicated by the event—would certainly have been re-garded then as mere vestiges of Tory prejudice. Whether today American opinion is quite as unanimous in the view that Mr. Chamberlain was right and Mr. Churchill wrong may be questioned.

American opinion today is of course primarily concerned with the bearing of the Indian question, first and last, on the fortunes of the war. Says a typical commentator: "Give India a rallying cry, freedom. The problem is not complicated if you apply the principles of democracy—majority rule, minority's protection from injustice. In India's case the majority are 250,000,000 Hindus, the minority 80,-000,000 Moslems."

If, indeed, it were as simple as that, there would be no problem. If Britain moves with caution towards doing in India what she has already done in the case of the Dominions, it is, at least in part, be-cause what one section in India regards as independence and freedom, other sections would regard as gross betrayal by Britain of interests and rights she had pledged herself to defend. To ignore this is to run the risk of something like civil war in India, of under-mining gravely the morale of the Indian Army, already a million and a half and potentially very much greater. This writer heard a Moslem say not long since: "If the government yields to Congress, I prophesy that half the men in the army will take their guns and go home." Perhaps he exaggerated.[1]

It is not true that the "minority" opposing the Congress Party are solely eighty million Moslems (the latest census, by the way, gives over ninety millions and many outside India would be affected). To these, also fiercely opposed to the Congress policy, must be added fifty million Untouchables, over five million Sikhs (mili-tarily important), and a good proportion of the people of the native states whose populations number eighty millions and whose rulers all strongly oppose Congress. These do not constitute a "minority," but something like half the population of India.

---

[1] Yet Edgar Snow telegraphs from India in September (1942): "In conversa-tion with me Jinnah (the Moslem leader) said: 'If the British were to agree to all the demands of the Congress, the Moslems would without doubt revolt throughout India.'"

The British government has declared repeatedly (as through the Viceroy in August, 1940) that it desires to see a constitution "drawn up by Indians in India" originating "from Indian conceptions of the social, economic, and political structure of Indian life" which Britain will accept and promote, subject only to one condition: "that it would not be repudiated by large or powerful elements in Indian national life."

Critics of the British case make much of Nehru's guarantees to the Moslems. But it no more meets the Moslem case to offer guarantees within a state predominantly Hindu than it would meet the Irish case to offer guarantees within a state predominantly British. The Irish could have had equality with Englishmen within a British state. They did not ask for equality; they asked for separateness, independence, on the ground that they made a separate corporate body, a nation. Moslems and others, far more distinct from Hindus than Irish are from English, make some similar claim as against Hindus.

It is true that no man has a right to ask complete justice in this world, and if unity and peace within India—and a more effective war effort—could be secured at the cost of minor injustices to Moslems or Untouchables, or Sikhs, or native states, one could ask their sacrifice with clear conscience. But if at this stage it is true that Moslems in India will no more accept constitutional subservience to a Hindu majority than the Jews in Palestine would accept constitutional subservience to a Moslem one, then the difficulty must be faced and overcome. It will not solve the problem nor aid the war effort to pretend that the facts do not exist.

The Faults of British Imperialism

For so very many progressives, Britain's maintenance of her imperialist position in India and elsewhere, and her hesitation to "free India," has been commonly attributed to mere financial avarice and rapacity. For a generation or more the heavens have rung with these denunciations of the unparalleled wickedness of British imperialism, the economic—capitalist—origins of which were deemed to be as certain as that turnips grew in the ground.

Of the fact that its main purpose was political, rooted in that same instinct of political self-preservation which prompted the Socialist Soviet Republics to launch wars of conquest against Finland and the Baltic Republics—of this, one can find in the usual Marxist invective not a trace. Yet it is quite clear that for Britain to risk civil war in India, thus laying the country open for invasion (as China was in some degree laid open by civil war) would amount to political suicide; suicide, not merely for Britain as a free state but for the young democracies of Australia, New Zealand, South Africa, to which British power and energy have given life.

British imperial rule has been marked by many and grievous faults; and a goodly proportion of this author's writing life has been spent in exposing those faults. But if we are not now to run into other errors as disastrous as any we have committed in the past, we must be clear what the faults really are. Of the course of policy during recent years we can say this: If the British imperialist had been a bit more imperialist in the sense of showing a greater regard for the defense of the Empire, than in fact he did show—we probably should not now be at war at all. He has been strangely indifferent to the effective defense of Empire; his faults have been mainly those of ineptitude and inertia; an indisposition to make the most of the opportunities for material and social development of the Empire; he has thought of himself too much merely as a policeman appointed to keep the peace between a lot of quarreling natives. Britain has failed to do what the circumstances of the world gave it such a great opportunity of doing: so to shape imperial policy as to identify the security of the British Commonwealth of Nations with the security of all free peoples throughout the world. Had the British actually done in the case of the Ethiopian matter, for instance, what they were so freely accused of doing by American critics—if they had used the League to maintain the status quo in Africa, using it, in other words, to keep Mussolini out of further encroachment on the Suez area—the Fascist aggressions might have been checked at an early stage. But British imperialists refused to do this, and preferred to deal with Mussolini, appease him, instead of opposing him.

It is commonly argued that colonial peoples like the Malays failed to fight because they had nothing to fight for. But the trouble throughout among the peoples that have become victims of Hitler is not that they refused to fight—the peoples of the Balkans, for instance, were ready enough to fight, as were the peoples of Finland and the Scandinavian states, as are the people of Ireland; but the nationalist bug has so eaten into them that they insist upon a form of separateness and independence which condemns them to impotent defenselessness however much they arm, however much they are prepared to fight. The Irish may have a grievance against the British and refuse to fight with the United Nations on that score. But the Norwegians and the Belgians and the Danes and the Dutch had no grievance against Britain, but nevertheless insisted upon the pursuit of a policy in the years preceding the war which made it impossible for them to fight effectively for their own defense, made it impossible for Britain or France effectively to aid them.

The Politics of the Military Offensive

One basic fact in the discussion is this: if the democratic world is to be able in the future to defend itself, our conceptions of the ethics of "independence" must be seriously revised. In the world of the eighteenth century, the world of vast distances, of oceans that took long months to cross, independence, almost complete and absolute, had a relation to freedom it no longer bears. Freedom today can no longer depend upon separation. If it is to survive it will be by virtue of organization, the co-operation of those who value it. And the new conditions may demand a new ethic. The strategic needs of the moment are already raising the ethical question in urgent form.

As these lines are being written the clamor everywhere is for the strategic offensive. We must take the offensive, we are told, or perish. But if we are to equal and beat the enemy in the effectiveness of his military offensive, the rapidity and sweep of his strategic initiative, we must equal and beat him in his political offensives too; one is impossible without the other. If we stand upon the political principles we have proclaimed heretofore, we cannot act with the promptitude of an enemy that does not admit neutrality. Recognition of this fact raises the question whether our attitudes, which happen to be militarily disastrous, are in truth the outcome of moral rectitude or moral confusion. In the interest of effective strategy now and effective postwar organization we should face the ethical questions even if we do not entirely answer them.

Recall the facts which have enabled the enemy at almost no military cost whatever to establish himself in vitally important strategic positions from which he can now be dislodged only at immense sacrifice of life. Quite early in the war Britain knew, everyone knew, that Germany would sooner or later, by an advance through the Low Countries and Scandinavia, attempt to outflank the Maginot Line and secure air and submarine bases upon the Atlantic for an attack upon Allied sea communications. The threatened countries were urged, implored, to co-operate with Britain and France in a well-prepared scheme of mutual defense. But the lesser states would have nothing to do with such plans. The very discussion of them, they urged, would imperil their neutrality; any partnership with a foreign state would compromise their national independence. The argument seemed to run that while refusal of Allied proposals would not provoke invasion by Britain or France, participation in them *would* provoke invasion by Germany. Allied scruples were already working enormously to Germany's advantage, in that the very knowledge of German aggressiveness was operating to prevent the building up of any effective resistance to it.

It is true that the Allies were told, as Britain is told by Eire today, that their help would be welcome after the German invasion had begun—but not one moment before. Yet it was quite clear to the least instructed that once invasion had begun, it would be far too late to send effective help. We know the outcome: Norway overrun in a few weeks, Holland in ten days; Denmark conquered by telephone; Belgium crushed in confusion and terror. Allied scrupulousness on the point of neutrality did not save these countries; it helped to destroy them. There is something tragically comic in the fact that the British forces which now, as Commandos, raid the Norwegian coast and are hailed in every Norwegian heart as an earnest of deliverance from Satanic tyranny, would have been fought as enemies if they had preceded the Germans by twenty-four hours, or long enough to take over the harbors the Germans now occupy and to mine and fortify them. Had the forces (which now, after disaster, are welcomed with such joy) come in time to prevent disaster, they would have been fought by the Norwegians themselves in the name of national right, self-determination, independence, neutrality, freedom. As a result Norway has for the time being lost all rights whatsoever, personal and national alike. It has lost them because like others, including Britain and America, it stood by a certain concept of political right which, if maintained by the nations generally, would make the defense of any right a physical impossibility, a concept which has indeed already put the nations of Continental Europe at Hitler's mercy.

The end of the story is not yet. For things may so develop that the whole issue of the war may turn upon the promptitude with which a Dakar, a Tunisia, a Martinique, a Portuguese or a Spanish island is occupied—or a De Gaulle recognized—and the enemy forestalled. (It was reported recently that at one moment a British force could quite easily have forestalled the Japanese in Thailand, but that the British commander did not dare to move for fear of sharp reproof from the home government, which had been emphatic in its insistence that Britain's record must be kept free of any charges of "aggression.")

The nature of the confusion which is still playing its part in hamstringing Allied offensive strategy is illustrated by a recent editorial comment of the *Saturday Evening Post's* (prior to Pearl Harbor) on a letter of Bernard Shaw's anent the problem of the Irish bases. Shaw felt impelled, as an Irishman, to testify that England had stuck to its bargain about Irish independence "as no other country in the world would have done." He pointed out that "Mr. de Valera is asking Mr. Churchill to imperil his forty million people for the sake of the mere paper neutrality of four million hostile Irishmen." (Had Shaw been writing after Pearl Harbor he might have added to the forty million imperiled British a couple of hundred million in the Americas, twice that number in China and the Antipodes, a similar number in India.) Ireland, insisted Shaw, could not be made another Switzerland, adding: "Mr. de Valera says those ports belong to Eire, but the day is gone when any race of people can call its land its own. Those ports belong to Europe, to civilization."

To which the *Post* replied:

If four million Irishmen have no rights that forty million Englishmen are bound to respect, what rights have forty million Englishmen that eighty million Germans are bound to respect? If the day is gone when people may call their land their own, what is England defending, and what is the war about? Thirdly, if this is liberal ethic and liberal thinking, then liberalism of this cult, as we have suspected before, is morally and intellectually bankrupt.

If the Allies, including America, had in fact and in all cases stood by the principle that the *Post* invokes in behalf of Ireland, the Allied cause would already have been lost. It has been expedient to be scrupulous in respecting the neutrality of Eire, despite the cost in ships and food and lives. But we can hardly pretend that there has been quite the same scruple in the case of Iceland, Greenland, Egypt, Syria, Iraq, Iran, or in the prewar years Panama, or, still earlier, in the case of a long list of British bases stretching from Gibraltar to the Far East. Suppose the same scruples had been observed. What would have been the result today? There can be no doubt whatever that if the American and British people had been as moral as all that, or had been moral in that particular fashion, a Nazi *Gauleiter* or a "Vichy" government would now be ruling in Britain, and every British port, every factory, and most of the British Fleet would be in Nazi hands; Africa and India would have fallen long since, and their teeming millions would have been made into tools of Nazi world domination.

Have we, then, been saved from that fate, at least for the time being, by sheer political immorality and wickedness? And do the present battle cries of independence and self-determination and national freedom mean that the organization of the general defense of the nations against a new violence, like that which Hitler has launched, must always be subject to the self-determination of a Gibraltar or an Aden—or an Eire? That the defense of civilization as a whole must always give way to the objection a state may raise to the presence of a foreign naval or air base upon its territory? That the one political impulse which must never be overridden and must always be regarded as sacred is the impulse to isolationism? In that case the future is with Hitler—the present Hitler or another—however this war may end.

The obviousness of this truth—that the Hitlers will always be able to pick off their enemies one by one, and the war fail of its prime object, if we accept our present battle cries at their face value—can hardly be regarded as favorable to a dauntless morale. True, we talk of a new League of Nations, the blueprint of which is presumably going to be so dazzling that nations will discard those emotions of nationalist separatism which we still foster, and which at present no one seems to have the courage to challenge, even to the extent of suggesting with any bluntness that we cannot possibly hope to render national rights secure until we have recognized and accepted the obligations by which alone the rights can be defended.

The difficulties of co-operation between independent states is not a new story; it is as old as the failures of Greek city states to achieve it. It is obviously one of the most difficult of all the tasks undertaken by men. If human experience anywhere gives any hint of forces which help toward success in that task, we ought to be ready to use those forces.

The Service of the "Dominion Idea"

The League of Nations failed to solve the fundamental problem of mutual aid in resistance to aggression; the members feared, and evaded, the responsibilities of collective defense. They preferred neutrality. But the nations of the much-criticized British Commonwealth—into which so large a part of the Empire has been resolved —did not fail in this particular, and the fact is mentioned here because actual events illustrate a political principle that it is vital just now to understand.

Although Canada, Australia, New Zealand, and South Africa had an independence which entitled them to be neutral, none of them chose that course. They were active belligerents more than two years before the United States became one. And it is worth while putting bluntly to ourselves the question: What would have happened if the Parliament of Canada, like that of Eire, had voted for neutrality? Would the fact that a "British" nation on this hemisphere decided to remain out of the war have had no effect on the development of American opinion, on President Roosevelt's task and course, on his two years' fight against isolationism? And could Britain have faced the enemy in Europe alone during more than a year if the Dominions had repudiated any obligation to come into the fight?

Why did they come in? Why did collective security, which in the case of the members of the League failed so egregiously, succeed in the case of half-a-dozen nations by no means entirely British, which included important French and Dutch elements?

A partial explanation is to be found in two facts: Although Britain has laid no statutory obligation on the Dominions, it has freely offered them the protection of British power—of the Navy, the naval bases, and the coaling stations scattered throughout the world. To accept or benefit by that help obviously involved a corresponding obligation—to give help in return. The obligation has been recognized in the retention by the Dominions of a mere symbol, the crown. Co-operation for security was made a reality by the existence of power at a center, coupled with the recognition that co-operation depended upon the acceptance of reciprocal obligations.

If the United Nations are to fulfill their task, centrally directed power must in this case also be freely offered as the means of security for all those co-operating, in return for their acceptance of the relevant obligations. With the accent on obligation. And of course coercion of those who repudiate the obligation cannot be excluded. No workable human society, no building up of law, has been possible without coercion, a coercion which need not endanger the purposes of the war if we know what we are doing and are not trapped by fallacies similar to those embodied in the *Saturday Evening Post* editorial referred to above.

That passage, with its cocksureness, is worth quoting if only to show how liberalism when applied to the field which now concerns mankind more than any other, the international field, has failed to explain itself to certain very important sections of the public. What has liberalism been doing all these years if the editor of the (then) most widely disseminated magazine in America can consider such an appeal as Shaw's for the fulfillment of obligations indispensable to the defense of any right for anybody, equivalent to the denial of right? Or if it is necessary to explain that anyone who wishes to be sure of calling his land or his property or his soul his own must make his contribution to the apparatus of defense—pay his taxes for police and courts and what not in the domestic field, and fulfill obligations even more onerous still in the too-long-neglected field of international relations?

Surely it ought not to be necessary at this date to explain that there is a difference between the criminal violence of an individual entering a man's house, killing its owner, and seizing it for the criminal's own evil purposes, between that and the seizure of property under the rule of eminent domain, by virtue of which alone at times the human community can defend itself, can uphold the law which prevents robbery and which alone makes either freedom or order possible.

Hitler's most powerful ally, the very basis of his victories, has been the ease with which he could divide his enemies by playing upon the dislike and distrust of one nation, or race, or religion, or party for another. Particularly have two "hates" served him; anti-Semitism and Anglophobia. He is still making immense use of them. To meet this danger we must face it, study it, understand it, not deny its existence; must admit our liability to this kind of infection, our tendency to seek devils to hate as an emotional relief, and scapegoats to blame as a means of escape from recognition of our own faults and obligations.

CHAPTER IX

Escapegoatism[1]

THIS book has been dealing largely with certain irrationalisms in human affairs which help to explain the world's present plight. For instance: Though the main conscious motive of a nation, as of other living things, is self-preservation, the determination to defend its life, yet all nations virtually without exception, save for sporadic, brief, and ineffectual efforts, have resolutely refused to fulfill the one condition by which alone self-preservation, defense, might become effective; that condition being co-operation with each other for common action against armed violence. They have refused to do collectively what each was ready to do individually.

We have seen each nation willing, for its defense, to expend its substance in armament, to sacrifice its wealth, to surrender the freedoms of its peoples' lives, to see the flower of its youth swept away and destroyed, to face agonies and torture beyond all power of words to describe. All these things have we seen men suffer for the safety of their country. But they would render it all vain, have the homes destroyed, the young men die, and the children disemboweled to no purpose, see their country pass into slavery, rather than have truck with foreigners, the people, that is, across the river, or the channel, or the hills; surrender the delight they seem to find in keeping alive some ancient feud; or their obvious pleasure at being able to impute evil intention, bad character, nefarious plots to the foreigner, of whatever kind.

And so we have said: "Let us fight, but only for ourselves, each for himself alone." And that, of course, has put all in peril of an evil

---

[1] This is not an attempted play upon words. To restore a word familiar in its abbreviated form to its completer and older form sometimes helps to remind us of implications commonly overlooked.

minority that does know at least how to gang up against this vast divided bulk and so is able to subdue it in detail. Of course it was not, is not, our intention to render these tragic sacrifices vain. A given nation does not say: "Let us send our young men to their deaths, although of course since we are eight million and the enemy eighty it will be to no purpose so far as the defense of the country is concerned." Things don't happen that way in the minds of men.

We declare that it is our duty to defend our country to the death; and are sincere. It is pointed out (taking the case of a European lesser state) that since eight cannot defend themselves against eighty we must have allies. Again, as an abstract proposition we may agree, though we are apt to leave it in the region of abstract truth. And then, in some entirely different context, which does not on the surface seem to have much relation to defending the country, certain dislikes, hates, prejudices arise. There are troublesome strikes. Communists are supposed to be at the bottom of them, "taking their orders from Russia." Feeling is aroused against Russia, and becomes deep and fixed. Then, when some arrangement for defense with her is suggested, the idea is indignantly rejected, the proposition about the need for allies being then conveniently forgotten, smothered in our indignation at the wickedness of Bolshevists. Or it may work somewhat differently. The French perceive that Germany, who has overrun their country twice before in the memory of men still living, seems to be getting ready for another thrust, as part of a program of European domination. Yes, France must be ready: a fact duly going into one compartment of the mind. Then the French read that Britain wants French help to prevent Mussolini from conquering Ethiopia and straddling the Suez Canal. "*Sacrebleu*, what is Ethiopia to us? The Suez Canal—why, Britain stole it from the French and now wants us to defend it for her! A very British proceeding. The lion does not change his spots. Unless we are very careful we shall go on fighting Britain's wars forever." So that when a little later Mr. Goebbels, who has great interest in the working of the average Frenchman's mind, puts out certain slogans throughout

France such as: "This is Britain's war," "Britain will fight to the last Frenchman," his seeds fall on fruitful soil. There is hesitation this time in resisting Germany's thrust; doubt, halfheartedness. The Right is disposed to be anti-British and the Left, with seventy-two Communists in the Chamber, disposed to be doubtful, because Russia is holding back. The doubts, the hesitation, the halfhearted-ness are prolonged even into the period of the war itself—and pre-pare the way for the final surrender.

In undermining the will to resistance in their victims the Nazi authorities never made the mistake of attempting to present a case for Germany. To persuade Frenchmen of the rightness of the Ger-man cause, to get them consciously to support it, would have been a task impossible of accomplishment. But to persuade them that they were against Britain was relatively easy because embers of old historic differences and hates still remained. Hitler knew that if these old differences could be made the means of preventing really effective co-operation, so that France could be separated from Brit-ain and both from Russia, then all three might be overcome. The Nazi knows that it is so much easier to induce men to act upon animosities, resentments, hates, than it is to get them to act on behalf of some common interest. To recognize a common interest demands almost always a considerable process of detached reasoning. But to allow animosities and resentments to guide us, demands no effort of self-discipline; only an easy yielding to the most ancient of animal impulses. ("The dogs fought because they did not like each other's smell.") Hitler knew—so very, very well—even when he first entered politics, that the quickest way to secure support for himself and opposition to some other, was to express some deep ancient tribal hostility, sure to be sleeping somewhere in the nature of his hearer. That is why he made anti-Semitism one of the main political tools in his whole bag of tricks. He knew, when he set about the destruction of the relatively democratic Weimar Republic, that he did not have to give any evidence to support his statement that the miseries of Germany were all due to the Jews; that the Republic had sold out to the Jews and that the Jews were selling out to the foreigner. The mere discovery of a tangible devil to explain it all, a scapegoat, someone, concrete and visible, upon whom to blame things, was, to a public heretofore puzzled and confused, not knowing who or what was to blame, an immense emotional release. They now at least knew their enemy; their tempers, their angers, at the way things were going, had found an outlet.

This process of divide and rule, by which Hitler has triumphed, would not have been possible save for the tendency among men to find some obscure and elusive pleasure in dislike of persons or groups that are "different," foreign, not of our tribe, or color, or race, or nation; and to take pleasure in insistence upon the difference; or in keeping alive some ancient grudge. It would seem that we dislike to give up a really satisfying hate; that we take pleasure in it.

The Jew in this connection is the ancient and classic example. No one has ever yet adequately analyzed or explained anti-Semitism. But certain obvious facts of this strange phenomenon suggest conclusions—warnings—which have a very direct bearing upon our problem of maintaining that inter-Allied unity, now become completely indispensable for the defeat of Hitler.

For two thousand years the Jew has been disliked, disliked so that even in this free and liberal and tolerant, and highly civilized America hotel managers hope to attract custom by announcing in a disguised phrase that Jews will not be admitted. What is the cause of this ancient and universal dislike? We speak of certain qualities of the "Jew." But Jews differ from each other so much that it would be as reasonable to talk of the qualities of people who live in houses bearing even numbers. To choose the Jew as the object of the dislike of the whole of Christendom—of the religious world which takes its name from Christ—is the more strange in that Jesus Christ was a Jew, His Mother was a Jewess, His twelve apostles were Jews, while the Holy Books of the Christian Faith, Old and New, are Jewish writings. To say of the people—if we *are* to talk in terms of race—which gave us Jesus Christ and His Mother and the Apostles, the Ten Commandments, and the basis of the moral law of Western civilization, that they have moral qualities we find distasteful, is indeed to raise the question of what qualities cause this world-wide hate.

But is it any quality of the Jew at all? You may find strong anti-Semitism among thousands who have never in their lives seen a Jew. A fashion of anti-Semitism will suddenly seize an area, like parts of the South that happen to have caught the Ku Klux Klan microbe. Thousands of honest folk, who never in this world have been injured by a Jew or even known one, will suddenly begin to rampage against Jews as vilely as Streicher himself. They put "the Jew" in the same category as the Pope o' Rome and the Nigger. There are other districts in which the Jew would not come into the favorite hate at all. If the real cause is in the quality of the Jew how comes it that those qualities change as he moves from one state into another?

What has the Jew to do in order that anti-Semitism shall end? What detail of conduct must he change, what quality modify? No one, of course, could say. And if the necessary changes of behavior or character, whatever they may be, *could* be made; if the immense majority of Jews who come into contact with the nations of the West made such changes, it would not dissolve anti-Semitism, or its use by Ku Klux Klanism or by Fascism throughout the world. For Ku Klux Klanism or Fascism derives immeasurably more from qualities within the Klansman or the Fascist than from qualities within the Jew.

Well, it is argued, however stupid, irrational these tribal hates may be, they are part of human nature; and in the mild form we know they may not do much harm. After all, it is no great matter that some people should prefer to spend their summer holidays where there are no Jews.

So argued for many years the decent Germans. Anti-Semitism in Germany has always existed, but, as any German of 1910, 1920, 1930, would have pointed out to you, Jews played an exceedingly important part in the life of the nation: in science, in commerce, in publishing, in the theater, music, literature, art. Anti-Semitism was anodyne.

Then Hitler decided to use it as a political instrument. Whereupon the world discovered that this mild prejudice, this tepid dislike, the thing that had heretofore expended itself in harmless music hall jokes, could be turned into something which in the hands of young ruffians became the justification for making elderly professors clean out lavatories with their hands; for stripping them naked in the frost and throwing cold water over them; for beating them to death with rubber truncheons; for kicking old women in the belly; for concentration camps, for deportations, for Polish ghettos, for infamies of bestiality and torture such that all the dreary history of man's monotonous cruelties leave the story unsurpassed. And however mild the anti-Semitism of those who did not wear Brown Shirts, it was enough to enable them to find excuses for acquiescence; for refusing to take the risks of protest.

Anti-Semitism was part of Prussian folklore and it lay under the skin of many Germans who were not Prussians. With the result that it furnished Hitler an extremely convenient weapon. When the harassed small businessman of Germany was told by Hitler, "You are being ruined by the Jews who have the government in their pockets," the suggestion fell on soil already prepared by casual remarks they had heard all their lives ("These damned Jews . . ."), to which they had paid no particular attention at the time, but which inevitably had left their effect. It was a comforting suggestion that Germany's troubles were due, not to any shortcomings of the Germans as a self-governing people, but to the presence among them of a beastly alien race who had betrayed their hosts, and who had managed to get power over the government; they and the government alike ought to be cleared out and if this fellow Hitler would do it, they were for him. That is how the thing went. That this form of demagogy made part of the general Hitlerian technique, there can be no doubt at all.

America, so far as anti-Semitism is concerned, is neither so inert nor so quiescent. The healthy body of this nation is reacting against the poisons of racial discrimination and hate. It is reacting alike against the disease and against the fatalistic doctrine that the disease is inevitable because "natural." Yellow fever is "natural" since the germ-bearing mosquito is part of nature. But we prefer to keep what he carries out of our blood. All newspapers of the better type, the best leaders of both parties, fine journalists like Ralph Ingersoll, put the challenge up to Americans to impose upon themselves the obligation to discipline these old obscure atavisms. And there is every sign that that movement is succeeding.

But so far this effort at social and political prophylaxis has not embraced very markedly "the ancient grudge" against the British within its scope. While public anti-Semitism is no longer tolerated in America, while articles or speeches in criticism of the Jews are commonly greeted with roars of protest, the kind of comment which, if the subject were Jews or Jewry, would be instantly condemned, provokes very little protest indeed if the subject be the British or Britain.

This is the more striking because many sections of the American public and press, and American commentators, have extended to Britain a generosity of testimony—and on the part of the American public as a whole a generosity of assistance and gifts—without precedent or parallel in international relations. Never before perhaps has such a flood of material assistance poured from the private citizens of one country to another, as that which poured from this country to Great Britain during the years 1940 and 1941; never before have citizens of one nation expressed so freely and so generously their admiration for the conduct of the citizens of another as American public men, writers, journalists, expressed for the conduct of the British during those years. And never before has there been greater boldness of leadership in a policy which meant the salvation of Britain than that which this nation received from its leaders during the dark year when Britain held the fort alone. Those things—apart from any other consideration—are too vivid in the minds of British people for occasional expression of Anglophobia to have any effect at all upon British public opinion. That is not now and in recent years never has been the important aspect of this subject. Its importance arises from the fact that the habit of Anglophobia, or political tail twisting, tolerated (by very many who do not really share the sentiment behind it) because it has become almost part of American tradition and folklore, does perpetuate a distorted view of British tendencies and policies which will add to the difficulties of a co-operation that is going to be difficult in any case. The last thing that this writer would dare attempt is a defense of the likability of "the Briton" (whoever he may be). These charges of arrogance, an unpleasant accent, and foolish and objectionable social habits may all be true. But adults ought not to discuss the kind of problem which now faces the two countries in those terms. We do not raise such matters when it is a question of co-operating with the Chinese, or Russians, or Czechs, or Greeks; they need not be raised in these other political decisions.

It is not a question of Americans having to "like" the British or the British the Americans. There is an element of myth or fantasy in this whole business of international likes or dislikes. You cannot "like" fifty or a hundred and fifty million people, because you will never see them, never can see them; do not know whether they, or which of them, are likable or not. It is, again, like asking whether you prefer those who live on the north sides of streets to those who live on the south sides.

The British have no traditional liking for the French; indeed France was for centuries Britain's traditional foe; there has never been any "blood thicker than water" business or "hands across the Channel" between them. Particularly had they no reason to like the "French" at the moment that their premier asked to be released from his promise not to make a separate peace, and the cabinet was contemplating surrender. Yet it was to this people at that moment that Mr. Churchill offered complete political union; offered to make Britain part of the French state—or France part of the British; to combine the two; to associate France's future indissolubly with that of Britain's. Churchill, who is an English patriot if ever there was one, with a deep sense of all that England's past means, made that offer, not because his people "loved" the French but because he believed that that political development might save

Western civilization from the domination of a dreadful evil. Few Englishmen perhaps relished the idea of having in future to discuss their policies with people who did not even speak the English tongue, whose values and way of life differed so much in some respects from the British. Yet, whatever the differences, they would not have been allowed to stand in the way of this development.

The importance of this phenomenon of Anglophobia may be illustrated by the part it probably played in the kind of decision which faced France at that moment. Goebbels had done his work well. Darlan was not the only public man in France who found in "the British" rather than in "the Jews" the scapegoat upon whom to blame the misfortunes of France. The decision to surrender was made, as we know, by a very narrow majority. A few more votes shifted from one side of the scale to the other might have saved the day. And Anglophobia, like anti-Semitism, had its part in the decision; was part of the forces which determined the fate of France— and of Europe.

It is worth noting in this connection that in making his offer to France, Churchill knew that he would not have to face in his public a degree of Francophobia which would stand in the way of giving effect to the offer if it should be accepted. Although Britain's wars with France were renewed century after century; and although the final battle which defeated Napoleon is more than a third of a century nearer to our time than the battle in which America won her independence, Francophobia does not seem to have bitten so deeply into any section of the British public as Anglophobia does into some sections of the American public.

The difference perhaps is revealed in this: If before the war there had existed in France some movement toward much closer co-operation with Britain, even eventually to some form of political union, many Englishmen might have believed that very little would come of it. But it is quite certain that, speaking broadly, not a living Englishman would have felt any resentment about it; no one I am sure would have written a book to prove the existence of a deep plot on France's part to complete or reassert the Norman Conquest; nor would those Englishmen, even if they had been bankers occupying in Britain the position that the Morgans occupy in America, who favored closer co-operation between the two countries, have been accused of lack of patriotism, ready to betray the independence of their country for the favors of foreign aristocrats. Yet since France had just about the same population as Britain, and had a very great military tradition behind her, the chances of Britain's playing second fiddle in any Anglo-French combination were immeasurably greater than would be the chance of an America of a hundred and thirty million becoming the junior partner in any American-British combination.

If one examine the kind of book dealing with Anglo-American relations of which Mr. Quincy Howe's lively and entertaining *Britain Expects Every American to Do His Duty* is perhaps an outstanding example, certain common features are revealed. They include, commonly, a fierce indictment of Americans who seek either in their personal or financial contacts close relations with Britain. That in itself is regarded evidently, if not as treason, then as something reprehensible or contemptible. One asks in some wonderment, Why?

Side by side with this indictment of Americans who seek closer relations with English people, is the indictment of what is declared to be the English habit of extending lavish hospitality to visiting Americans of any distinction in their own country. Whole pages in some of these books are devoted to the sly tricks employed by the British aristocracy to beguile Americans into—into what? Into being generally favorable to a closer co-operation of the two countries.[2]

---

[2] Here are samples from Mr. Howe's book:

It's fun, of course, to be fooled by the British for a century and more, but it's more fun to know how the trick works. An extraordinary spectacle unfolds. We shall see almost the entire ruling caste in the United States obeying British orders with an eager servility that arises from the unique character of modern American society. We shall see that the relationship between America and England has no parallel in the modern world.

Ancestral ties of language, tradition, and blood exercise such an attraction upon the American ruling class that it adapts its own selfish interests—not to mention the interests of the country as a whole—to the needs and desires of the British Foreign Office.

If one starts with the assumption that this objective is in itself a crime, a result from which this country is bound to suffer, then some of these books have meaning. If however, it is assumed that in this closer co-operation a very wealthy America of a hundred and thirty millions is probably quite able to take care of herself in contacts with a relatively poor England of forty-five millions—if that is the underlying assumption, then these books have very little meaning indeed, for the very end which is indicted as dangerous and evil is the end which we must now attempt to achieve.

It is the unargued premise of these books which is so disturbing, the almost unconscious assumption that closer co-operation with Great Britain must be to the disadvantage of America; the assumption that if it can be shown that Britain desires this co-operation, then that of itself should be reason for America to reject it. Thus, Mr. Howe prints whole pages of British expressions of desire for collaboration with the United States as a grave warning to the reader of the "peril" in which the United States stands.

Many Americans, sincerely and passionately desirous of future peace and an orderly world, are perhaps unaware of the presence in their minds of this unargued assumption. In making that observation might I remind the reader once more that my half-century of contacts with America includes some five years as a migrant farm hand and cowboy, listening to the political arguments of the bunkhouse and the camp fire; and, at a later stage, includes contacts with two generations of university students, students drawn from practically every state in the Union. Nor is mine the impression of an isolated witness. Canadians who are geographically in a good position to judge, who, when visiting the United States, are almost always by virtue of their speech taken for Americans, have repeatedly made the same observation. The Canadian author John MacCormac, who acted for long as Canadian correspondent for important American papers, in his recent book [3] lays down and cogently supports two propositions, (1) "Nothing is now more certain than that the United States and Britain must join their forces, or both will go

---

[3] *America and World Mastery*; Duell, Sloan and Pearce.

down"; and (2) "Powerful elements in American opinion will oppose such unity." In support of the latter proposition he testifies
that "there is tremendous resistance in the United States to co-
operation with England." He declares that if the proposed co-
operation were with France the resistance would be less.

A page or two back it was suggested that Anglophobia and anti-
Semitism belonged to the same family of psychological phenomena.
If one take typical passages from books about the British by authors
like Mr. Theodore Dreiser, or certain editorials of the Hearst, Mc-
Cormick, or Patterson press; or certain speeches made in Congress
within the last year or two, and change the word "British" to "Jews,"
one would get expressions of anti-Semitism not much less vivid than
those which you would find in the pages of the German anti-
Jewish Press.[4] Some of those critics have in the recent past dilated
with very great freedom upon the offensive qualities of the British
character, the arrogance of the British, the sly bad faith of their
diplomacy, the selfishness and bad faith of British traders, the
rapacity of British imperialism, the oppressive character of British
colonialism. They assume an inevitable conflict of interest between
this country and Britain, and attribute to Britain plots as nefarious
as those which the professional anti-Semite attributes to the
Elders of Zion, or the professional anti-Catholic to the Pope. We
should all be shocked if anything at all similar were said of Jews.

Of course the two cases are not on the same plane. Britain is a
political entity, which the Jews are not, and is responsible for policies
which affect America; Britain's bad colonial management, or mis-
management, say, in India, may imperil the very defense of the

---

[4] Thus, Mr. Hearst in his syndicated column four months after Pearl
Harbor, writes:
England has systematically sacrificed her Allies to her own safety and her own
immediate objectives. She sacrificed Norway—withdrew from the battlefront
without informing the Norwegian forces. . . . She sacrificed Belgium in iden-
tically the same manner.
England abandoned France at Dunkirk and executed a masterly retreat to
England. The French term it as "masterly" desertion of the Allied cause. . . .
England's policy is to have allies but not be an ally.
A nation can render any aid or service to England it pleases, but it must not
expect any aid and service in return.

United States itself. Americans, therefore, have every right and obligation to criticize.

Criticism of "the British" in this connection is justifiable because
they stand for an organized state, a political corporation, with which
America proposes to make a bargain; and the Jews don't stand in that
relationship at all. But if the Jews did represent a world empire whose
downfall would make American defense much more difficult, that
fact obviously would not make anti-Semitism in America less dangerous, it would make it more dangerous. In the present crisis of
civilization the survival of democracy, of the parliamentary kind
common to nations like the United States, Australia, New Zealand,
Canada, Britain, may well depend, almost certainly will depend,
upon the capacity of the United States and Great Britain to co-
operate without too much friction while indulging in fairly free
criticism. Yet, that being the situation, ought it to be regarded as
venial, quite "safe" on the part of a politician to indulge in a degree
of anti-American, or anti-British innuendo and abuse (as the case
may be) which directed at Jews or Catholics or Irish or Christian
Scientists would not only be deeply reproved by public opinion, but
would be politically extremely dangerous for the critic?

Just because British imperial policy is now, and will be more and
more, of very direct concern to America, and must be subject to
American criticism, it is necessary to put the discussion on a plane
from which "phobias" on both sides have been abolished.

The British in this matter are placed in a curious dilemma. They
are sometimes counseled by American friends not to present the
British case at all because, coming from Englishmen, it might be
resented. "Let the facts speak for themselves." But obviously the
facts have not spoken for themselves when it is possible for a very
powerful newspaper editor to blame Britain for "holding on to the
gold mines of the Transvaal" when, in fact (as pointed out in a
previous chapter of this book) they were transferred to an independent government thirty years ago. But apart from that, when it
is a question of indicating the desires or intentions of Britain, it is
better obviously that Britons should speak.

In this matter there can hardly be any doubt of the desires and intentions of Britons. A long line of public men, of which Mr. Churchill is merely the last, have declared the desire of Britain "to march side by side with the United States in majesty and in peace."

From the American side there are commonly two types of objection, one political, the other related to what we are told are the objectionable personal qualities of the British.

On the first count we are told that America would not stand for British imperialism. On examination (but not until examination) it is admitted that so far as the Dominions are concerned we are not dealing with an Empire at all. As to the dependent Empire and India, I am quite sure that any British government, as part of securing effective co-operation with the United States, would be prepared to say: "If you indicate how, under a purely Indian government set up during war time, we shall not run the risk of repeating the experience we have had with Eire, or with France, we are prepared to follow your indications. The motive in our retention of India bears mainly upon this problem of defense which is yours as much as ours."

Further, I have no doubt whatever that, so far as the members of an American administration are concerned, grounds of agreement could be found. The difficulty would come with a public opinion acting under the impulsion of words, slogans, generalizations, stemming from a long-sustained tradition of mistrust of Britain.

That mistrust and dislike bear upon the second objection, namely, the objectionable personal qualities of the British, their "haughtiness," arrogance, patronizing airs. . . .

As to that, one is brought back to the point noted earlier in this chapter in relation to anti-Semitism: anti-Semitism is sometimes most acute with those who have never seen a Jew. Of the millions of the Middle West (where Anglophobia is supposed to run strongest) what proportion are ever brought into contact with Englishmen of their mental picture? Their feelings are the result of tradition, legend, suggestion.

And what are Englishmen to do about it?

If nine hundred and ninety-nine out of a thousand behaved well there would always be a thousandth who did not; and the misbehavior of the thousandth would be enough to keep the old legends alive.

And would either of us pay any attention at all to these bickerings if we had any sense of the gravity of the situation which confronts both alike? In asking that question I have in mind an incident in France during the period of the "phony" war, when so many French had become thoroughly bored and irritated with everything connected with the struggle. Talking with a Frenchwoman I had known for years I found her vaguely and ill-temperedly anti-British. Why? Well, British officers had been billeted in her home in France; they had been, she said, ill-mannered, noisy; monopolized the bathroom, were always making tea in the kitchen. The British in fact were an objectionable people. "And so," I suggested, "you are opposed to the British alliance?" Well, not opposed to it, *but* . . . and I saw that the soil had been well prepared for the seed of Nazi propaganda. True, she did not want the Boche to win, but her state of irritation "at British manners" predisposed her to receive willingly the Nazi suggestion that perhaps France was being made to pull British chestnuts out of the fire, and to accept the Nazi slogan that Britain would fight to the last Frenchman, and so on and so on. And out of these vague resentments—which I knew had for some years before the war been sedulously cultivated among millions of ordinary French people like my friend—came hesitations, waverings, a moment of faltering morale; a moment of which the Germans made the most—with results we know.

There is a sequel to that story which is its main point.

The British officers went away from my friend's house; and the Germans came to the town where it was situated. And now, after many months, news of this French lady has filtered through to her friends in Britain. At dawn one day the Gestapo men came and seized her and her daughter and young son . . . and took them away, no one knows where, of course, for "questioning," on the charge of sheltering British officers and RAF pilots. Her house, the

German authorities charged, had become a station on the under-ground railway by which English soldiers and the Free French found their way to Britain. This Anglophobe, she who, because British officers had sung in her bathroom and cluttered up her kitchen, had not been particularly keen on British victory, had discovered in the hour of her country's tragedy that she was ready to risk her life—she may by now have given it—and the lives of her children, to give shelter to these detestable people, to the end that Britain's triumph might make possible the liberation of France. And if she still lives she probably lives for the day when British officers will once more rudely sing in her bathroom and make tea in her kitchen.

The point of such a story is surely clear enough. Isolationism may be right (there are quite respectable arguments for it); co-operation may be right—that case has been argued in the preceding pages; but what cannot possibly be right is for either party to let the issue depend upon resentments caused by the rudeness of a visiting Briton or American as the case may be; depend upon our irritation at the Oxford accent or the American; upon whether a British journalist did or did not once call Uncle Sam Uncle Shylock; or even let decision be determined by the fact that remote ancestors of the present-day English (who, incidentally were just as much ancestors of Washington, and Jefferson, and Jackson, and Lincoln) were guilty of brutalities in Ireland, three hundred years ago.

That the British people depend upon American co-operation for their very survival is evident on the face of things. They make no secret at all of their need of such co-operation, of their plain interest in American good will toward them. On simple grounds of interest therefore they are likely to be ready to do what can be done to ensure American good will, to help on their side bury ancient hatchets, to forget the ancient grudge.

What *can* they do?

There are certain things that no free nation can do. That silly journalists will occasionally write silly things about America in the British press is inevitable. Nothing but a tightly organized censorship of opinion along Nazi lines could possibly prevent it. And such controls in peacetime are not in the British any more than in the American habit, nor is it possible to prevent foolish remarks by a visiting Englishman. One rude or foolish individual in a hundred is enough to cause the hundred to be condemned. In some circumstances, if one wants to perpetuate the memories of old animosities, one fool in a million is enough to supply the necessary fuel for the flames of collective dislike or hate.

In his early wanderings in this country the present writer came to know fairly intimately a good many farming families, living in remote districts, as well as ranch hands, cowboys, miners. He encountered everywhere great friendliness to himself, not infrequently on the ground that he was "so different from other Englishmen." But again and again it happened that a little questioning brought out the fact that this one was the only Englishman they had ever encountered. But long before they had met an Englishman in the flesh they had a picture of "the" Englishman—supercilious, arrogant, offensive. The fact that they had never before seen an Englishman did not in the least prevent them from forming that definite picture, and carrying throughout their lives a dislike based on it.

But I encountered a fact stranger still. In later years I had occasion to travel through the South. And there commonly I found no such picture of "the" Englishman. Southerners seemed not to have heard that Englishmen were arrogant, supercilious, self-satisfied, snobbish, absurd, offensive. On the contrary I was told repeatedly that "in the South we like the English; the Englishman is very popular." But if the Northern, or Western, or Middle-Western picture had any basis in actual fact, must we assume that "the" Englishman suddenly changes his character immediately he crosses the Mason and Dixon line?

When therefore we hear that Anglophobia in America is due to "the" Englishman's characteristics, we know that those characteristics, even if they are as described above, have probably very little to do with the matter.

History has a good deal more to do with it. In the earliest vital struggle in which America was engaged the enemy was Britain and the enemies were British. That gave an early twist to thought about the outside world, a twist perpetuated by schoolbook history, which has remained ever since, although it is clear that the gravest challenge to the "American way of life" has not come from the English but from Americans themselves. If the challenge of the Confederacy had been successful, if the Union had been smashed and a slave power firmly entrenched upon this hemisphere, then democracy and freedom would have received a mortal blow, as Lincoln well knew. Yet, although all Americans today know it to be wise to forget this graver challenge and the animosities of that time, know that it is a mischievous and evil habit to "wave the bloody shirt," the far older animosities of a far older struggle are sometimes allowed to simmer and get in the way of co-operations upon which now all freedom may depend.

Once more, what must the British do on their side to facilitate those co-operations?

One American friend to whom I put the question suggested that "the British must become more assimilable; must mix more readily." The friend who made the suggestion was a third-generation American. His father had been born here; his grandfather had been an immigrant—from Ireland. And he still called himself "Irish-American," which provoked certain reflections as to "British assimilability" with Americans. We know that for generations in American politics there has been not only an Irish vote, but a German vote, an Italian vote, a Polish vote, a Greek vote, a Catholic vote. But there has never been an English vote. Does this mean that the English element in the immigrations of the nineteenth century were so small in comparison with the Polish and the German and the Greek as to be negligible? But in fact those of English origin outnumbered those of any other single nationality. And if, as is sometimes charged, there is some "innate" hostility on the part of the English to the American, a British "plot" to influence American politics, we would at some time or other have had an English, just as we have had an Irish, or a Polish vote. But in fact there has never been this "separateness" of the English element in American politics or life. The other day in New York it was charged that "the Irish" were securing an undue proportion of jobs. But you have never heard of "the English" or an "English-American" getting this or that position. Some years ago in a Midwestern city a pageant of national groups was organized. It was easy enough to find a Greek Colony, a German one, an Italian or Polish, or Irish. But no English colony could be found. The English immigrants had been so completely absorbed into the body of American national life as to have disappeared as a separate entity. The English had become so American as to have vanished as an English group. And they were the only considerable national group so to have done.

In the old days we felt impelled to burn a man alive if he did not attend our church. Never, men were sure, could those of the true faith live at peace with heretics. But they found that men of different faiths could live together; that they could keep their differences, yet be loyal to each other in the achievement of their common purposes. Religion is not less than nationalism. What is possible in the one field is possible in the other.

The questions asked in the first chapter are here answered seriatim on the basis of the principles just discussed. A number of additional questions are also answered.

CHAPTER X

The Final Quiz

In the light, then, of the discussion of these pages, let us see what distinct answers are to be given to the specific questions which appear at the beginning of this book; and to other related ones which would certainly arise in John Citizen's mind as he considered the replies. Take the first:

Q. *This is a war to make the world safe for democracy. So was the last. But it did not do it. Why should this one?*

A. This war will not do it either unless we all do what none of us as nations did adequately after the last war—hang together to defend in common the right of each to national life, the right to be secure from destruction by aggression from outside. If in the future we allow our fellow nations to be picked off one by one, so that their resources can then be used against us by their conqueror, the new victory will be no more permanent than the last. This is not the only condition of a secure democracy, but it is the first and most indispensable.

Sumner Welles answered this question when he reminded us recently that the sacrifice made by those who died in the last war was rendered vain to the extent that their children had to travel the same dreadful road again, because we, the civilians who survived, did not do our part. "These ninety thousand dead, buried on the slopes of Arlington and in the fields of France where they fell in battle," he pointed out, "fulfilled their share of the bargain struck. Can we, the living, say as much? Can we truly say, on this Memorial Day, that we have done what we, as a nation, could have done to keep faith with them, and to prevent their sacrifice from being made in vain?"

He went on:

The people of the United States were offered at the conclusion of the last war the realization of a great vision. They were offered the opportunity of sharing in the assumption of responsibility for the maintenance of peace in the world by participating in an international organization designed to prevent and to quell the outbreak of war. That opportunity they rejected. They rejected it in part because of the human tendency after a great upsurge of emotional idealism to seek the relapse into what was once termed "normalcy." They rejected it because of partisan politics. They rejected it because of the false propaganda, widely spread, that by our participation in a world order we would incur the danger of war rather than avoid it. They rejected it because of unenlightened selfishness.

What Sumner Welles said of this country applies, of course, equally—allowance being made for special circumstances—to the countries of Europe as well. Isolationism is not simply an American disease; it arises from tendencies common to all the democracies of Western society, in Europe as much as in the Americas. "We are reaping," said Welles, "the bitter fruit of our own folly and of our own lack of vision. We are paying dearly as well for the lack of statesmanship, and for the crass errors of omission and of commission, so tragically evidenced in the policies of those other nations which have had their full share of responsibility for the conduct of human affairs during the past generation."

As to the way in which the previous failures are to be avoided Welles expressed his belief that the people at the end of the war would demand that the victorious nations join with the United States:

. . . to undertake forthwith during the period of the armistice the disarmament of all nations, as set forth in the Atlantic Charter, which "may threaten aggression outside of their frontiers."

I believe they will insist that the United Nations undertake the maintenance of an international police power in the years after the war to insure freedom from fear to peace-loving peoples until there is established that permanent system of general security promised by the Atlantic Charter.

Finally, I believe they will demand that the United Nations become the nucleus of a world organization of the future to determine the final terms of a just, an honest and a durable peace to be entered into after the passing of the period of social and economic chaos which will come inevitably upon the termination of the present war, and after the completion of the initial and gigantic task of relief, of reconstruction and of rehabilitation which will confront the United Nations at the time of the armistice.

And that, might add the persistent John, is all very well, but what of the imperialisms of the victors? Take, for instance, the next two questions:

Q. *Are our boys fighting in India, Burma, Ceylon, Africa to give those countries democracy, or to maintain the British Empire in those parts? Why are we defending that Empire in Australia and New Zealand and Africa and Ireland and many other places, when our forefathers fought to be free from it, and did their best to destroy it?*

A. America is not fighting to preserve those countries for the British Empire; she is fighting to prevent them falling into the hands of the Axis—Germany or Japan—so that they shall not become areas from which attacks may be launched upon the democratic world, and their resources used for America's destruction, now or in the future. In defending them America is not defending British imperialism. Australia and New Zealand are neither empires nor the oppressed provinces of an Empire struggling to be free. They are independent states that have grown into democracies as thoroughgoing as any, with social security systems and labor movements more advanced and developed than any others in the world. This has been possible because, in the years they were growing up and might otherwise have been exposed to Japanese or German interference, both Australia and New Zealand lived under the protection of British sea power. But for that power the story of these islands would have been very different. Before 1914, Germany owned Pacific territory uncomfortably close to Australia, and Japan was for long a threat to both. Neither country was compelled to make any contribution to the upkeep of that naval power by which small, remote settlements (in their early phases indefensible by means of their own strength against immensely powerful states that might otherwise have overwhelmed them), were able to grow into flourishing independent democracies as free and prosperous as any in the world.

As to India, Burma, Africa and other Asiatic and colored countries, self-government obviously has difficulties that do not present themselves in the case of a country like Canada or Australia. If conflicts between the races, religions, and castes in those countries create divisions which expose them to foreign invasion, we know now that the security of the United States itself is involved. Britain has hesitated to grant full self-government to India mainly because of fear about the security of the Commonwealth as a whole—particularly Australia and New Zealand. If the United Nations really stand as a defensive unit after the war it will be justifiable to take greater risks, and India is certain to become independent—an independence already promised by Britain; a promise which might perhaps be guaranteed by the United Nations, or some of them.

If you think it is a matter of indifference to this country's security what becomes of those distant territories, just imagine that by American refusal to help in their defense they passed into the hands of the Axis; imagine that Japan had established herself in the island continent of Australia (killing off its people if they became troublesome as systematically as the Germans have been killing off the people of Poland or Czechoslovakia); adding Australia to the already achieved conquest of Java, and other of the Dutch East Indies, Malaya, Burma, Indo-China. Whether India were left to Germany or Germany devoted herself to the exploitation of Russia, Persia, Iran, Syria, Egypt, Afghanistan, Arabia, and Africa, the fact would remain that something like four-fifths of the man power of the world would have passed into the hands of the Axis. Would you as an American citizen feel comfortable?

Q. *Does this mean that we have to go on defending the British Empire even after the war is over, indefinitely, as part of the peace settlement?*

A. You will have to go on defending—or continue taking your part in the defense of—India, Burma, Malaya, the Philippines, and China and other territories—as they will have to go on defending you. When we talk as though all the defending were all on our side do we not conveniently overlook what China has been doing for five years or more? At this writing (the middle of 1942) America is sending no appreciable material aid to China. Since the conquest of Burma and the closing of the Burma Road, there is no means of getting it to her. But if China were not fighting immense quantities of Japanese ammunition and material, great Japanese armies now absorbed in meeting the Chinese would be liberated for attack upon the United States and its allies like Australia. Suppose the Japanese had found in Chiang Kai-shek a Chinese Laval, and the resources of China were as open to Japan as those of France are to Germany? Is all the "defending" on one side?

The same consideration of course applies to American defense of the British Empire. If Britain had yielded or collapsed as France did, and complete command of the sea, as well as the command of Britain's industrial and shipping resources, had gone to Germany; and India had gone the way of Indo-China—what chances of final victory would the United States possess?

Q. *Is it not true, as a distinguished American has said, that this war has come because Britain owns too much of the world and others too little? Because Italy and Germany and Japan have neither enough raw materials nor sufficient outlet for their population? That it is a war between the Haves and the Have-nots? Is it not a gross injustice that Britain—a nation of forty-five million—should own a quarter of the earth?*

A. Britain does not "own" what we call the British Empire, and such a word used in this connection distorts our thought about the whole subject of war and its causes and cure, as the preceding pages have tried to show. If Canada, a "British possession," became part of the United States, the farms, houses, furniture, radios now in the hands of one set of owners would not be transferred to another set of owners. There would be a change of government, not a transfer of property. As to raw materials, the most important raw material of Canada is wheat. The Briton, who "owns" Canada, does not get the wheat for nothing; he has to pay for it like any Jap or German or Italian; and, except when these latter folk go to war, the Canadian is just as ready to sell his wheat to them as to an Englishman; it is just as available to them as to the British. So with other raw materials throughout the Empire. No one prevents the Germans or the Japs having "access" to them, for they are produced for the express purpose of being sold. It is true that the German or the Italian, just like the Briton, has to have money wherewith to pay for these goods and that he can only get the money by selling his own goods, and that high tariffs sometimes prevent his doing it and play havoc with his currencies. This is the form of "imperialism" which is the real obstacle to "free access to raw materials," a far greater obstacle than the political distribution of colonies, which, incidentally, do not happen to be the main source of raw materials. Yet this very real obstacle to effective distribution of raw materials is very rarely mentioned; and it happens to be an obstacle in the creation of which America has done her part.

The most notable Have-not nations are the lesser states of Europe —Finland, Norway, Sweden, Denmark, Switzerland. They had no colonies to "give" them raw materials, no *Lebensraum*, no guaranteed "access" to raw materials—and their peoples were the most prosperous in Europe, if not in the world; with a better standard of living than the people of either Britain (despite her "ownership" of Empire) or Russia, or Germany. Their economic position was as good as that of any Have nation. It was the weakness of their political—military—position, a weakness that only cooperation with others could have remedied, which accounts for the fact that their high standard and life and civilization, their prosperity, have all been changed to semistarved slavery.

The fallacy behind British "ownership" can be grasped perhaps by studying a suggestion made in the preceding pages. If the whole of the British Empire, lock, stock, and barrel, Britain as well as the colonies, were taken over by the United States so that the

United States became the "owner," no Briton would lose a pound, and no American gain one by the mere fact of transfer of "ownership." Benefits might accrue from the abolition of tariff walls (if they *were* abolished; for all British "possessions"—including India —are very jealous of their right to raise tariffs, a right which they very freely exercise even against Britain herself). But from the mere fact of change of "ownership" there would result virtually no transfer of property at all.

To say that Japan's position in China is comparable to that of Britain's in India, is to ignore every fact in the situation which most concerns the United States. Britain has been in India longer than she has been in Canada. Britain's position in India has no more threatened the United States than has her position in Canada. Furthermore, India has developed far-reaching parliamentary institutions under British rule: eleven provinces, where the governments are entirely Indian, now possess those institutions; there is a national Parliament at Delhi. India under British rule has developed far more of the institutions of Western democracy than China has developed as an independent state; India has developed them without civil war while China under the republic has known most devastating civil wars. India's parliaments are not the outcome of purely Indian culture; they are the outcome of Britain's position in India; have so far led India peacefully along the road toward democracy. To say that Britain's position in India threatens the United States as would the Japanese conquest of China; or that if Japan and Germany were to take Britain's place in India, it would make no difference to the security of this country, is to ignore the reality of what is now going on in the world: to show ignorance of what this war is about and why it has come upon us.

Q. *For years it has been commonly asserted that the European victors used the victory which American aid made possible, for their imperialist purposes, adding greatly to their territorial conquests. What assurance have we that that experience will not be repeated?*
A. The final settlements of this war will probably be made in Washington, with this country itself the most powerful of all the victors.

Moreover nearly all the others will be dependent upon America for food and money, let alone minor needs. It is altogether likely that the President of the United States will be the President of the Great Council of the United Nations. By virtue of this situation, veto power over final arrangements will pass into the hands of the United States if this country cares to use such power. The victor next in material importance to the United States is likely to be Great Britain, who will dispose of a great deal of shipping and manufacturing plants. Some of her chief sources of food and raw material will be such Dominions as Canada, Australia, New Zealand. With all of these the United States has direct and independent relations, relations, that is, not through Great Britain, but through independent ministers and agencies. Not only have Canada, Australia, New Zealand, and South Africa independent representatives in Washington, but an American general is in command of the defenses of Australia; American commissions are active in the organization of Indian defense industries; American financiers have an immensely greater stake in Canada than have British financiers.

Add to this that British governments, and most notably the government of Mr. Churchill, have, with the full concurrence of the Dominions, expressed repeatedly a desire for ever closer relations with the United States. It is rather America which holds back from closer ties. If Mr. Churchill could offer complete Union to France, offer to make Britain and France one country, an offer made when France was on the point of collapse, it is certain that he would be ready to offer, with the full concurrence of his people, a Union not less complete with this country. In which event the dominant voice in the future course of the Empire would be with America, not with Britain; America's voting preponderance would be as 130 to 45.

If in such a situation as that just described America acquiesces in a settlement too favorable to the other victors it would be because she did not deem it worth while to exercise her influence or her power.

Q. *Many students have maintained these last years that the power of financial interests supporting an astute British propaganda played a large part in involving us in the last war. Have those forces been at work in involving America in this war also?*

A. There is only one ultimate question of policy for Americans in this war: Is it vital to the security of this country that Germany and Japan should be defeated? If to that supreme question you answer "Yes, it *is* vital for the safety of this country that Germany and Japan should be defeated," then the fact that the defeat of those enemies will also add to the security of other free nations is not something which should be resented, but something at which we should all rejoice, because it provides the chance that others will fight with us, aid us in the common task, instead of remaining neutral or becoming an enemy.

Sometimes the charges about "British propaganda" would seem to carry the implication that if the British desire the defeat of Hitler and Hirohito then it must necessarily be something which is bad for the United States. We all now agree, however, that that defeat is something vital to the freedom of America. The British are accused of having tried to make that fact clear some time before it was clear to all sections in America; tried to induce this country to take the earliest possible action against the growing aggression. Ought the fact to excite much feeling beyond regret that the British were not a bit more successful, successful in accelerating American action in both cases? Their primary purpose was not—and to do the British justice they never pretended that it was—to "save America," any more than that the primary purpose of American aid was to "save Britain"; the purpose on both sides was common action for the defense of common interests, since the salvation of either depended upon the salvation of both. To assume, as so much of the criticism of "foreign" propaganda does assume, that if a given course benefits others it must necessarily be harmful to us, is an inverted altruism very common in politics—and very disastrous. "If to save ourselves we must save others, then let us perish" is a very strange but sometimes quite popular doctrine.

As a matter of simple fact, there has been exceedingly little British propaganda in America in the past and that little exceedingly

bad, as is proved by the British failure to make known to the great
mass of Americans such things as the real independence of the Dominions; the degree of "de-imperialization" referred to in a previous
chapter.

Britain sought American help in the last war, as in this, first of all
because without that help Britain would have gone under. It was
Britain's business to put that consideration first. It was America's
business to put first, if you will, considerations of American security,
and to ask whether the defeat of Britain by Hitler, the conquest of
Britain and the British Empire by the Axis, would endanger the security of the United States. If it would, then it was the job of
American statesmanship to aid in the defense of Britain as a measure
of American security. Without American help, or rather without
the prospect of it, Britain would almost certainly have been forced
ultimately to the dreadful course of France; might have been forced
to surrender, to create a Vichy government, to become an unwilling
instrument of the Axis; more helpless under Axis domination than
even France is. Would such a situation make for the security of
America? The question for Americans is not whether British resistance to the Axis is good for Britain, but whether it is good for
America and her security. Is it not just possible that what is good
for Britain may also be good for the United States?

Those who know the facts know that all the talk of a satanically
efficient British propaganda is a myth. British propaganda is about
the worst in the world. But if it were the best, its excellence would
still be a red herring, drawing attention from the real issue. The
issue for the American people is whether the defeat of the British
Empire (which even Lindbergh has described as something which
would be a "disaster for the whole world") and the substitution of
German domination for British, would endanger the United States.
That can be put to a quite simple test which has already been suggested in reply to a previous question. Ask even the extremest isolationist: Would he be prepared to see Germany occupying the harbors in Canada (on the Pacific as well as on the Atlantic seaboard),
in Newfoundland, in the West Indies, in Central America (British

Honduras, within two or three hours' flight of the Panama Canal), in British Guiana (also within easy flight of the Panama Canal), now occupied by naval forces of the British Empire? Would he be prepared to see Germany establish herself in positions of great strategic power on this hemisphere, in a position with command of the sea to send great German armies into Canada? All Americans know that this country would fight to prevent Germany establishing herself upon this hemisphere in any such position. But that is the position which Britain *has* occupied on this continent during the whole course of America's history. Not merely has Britain's position not endangered the United States, but such features of American policy as the Monroe Doctrine, to which this country has in the past attached great value, have been made possible only by the co-operation of Great Britain and the support of the British Navy. So little has the powerful strategic position of the British Empire on this hemisphere threatened this country that its land frontier, the longest land frontier of any country in the world, has been completely unfortified during more than a century and a quarter.

All this proves that we know by experience, by the plainest facts of history, that this country can live safely with the British Empire, even when the position of that Empire on this hemisphere is one of immense power. We know further that the United States would never permit a triumphant Germany that had conquered Britain so to establish herself upon this hemisphere at all; that this country would go to war to prevent such an outcome, if she had not gone already. In view of that quite undeniable fact, the fact that a British Canada, a British West Indies, a British Honduras, and a British Guiana are things Americans can live with and which do not threaten America; and that a German Canada, a German West Indies, a German Honduras, a German Guiana are things the American people do not believe they could live with in security; in view of that fact, the talk about Britain's propaganda and imperialism is clearly irrelevant. If there are features in the government of countries like Canada, or Australia, or New Zealand, or South Africa, or India, or Burma which Americans do not like, the growing influence of this country with Britain, and Britain's growing dependence upon American aid, will doubtless enable America to secure modification of those features. But the fact of such defects cannot possibly be a good reason for acquiescing in the exchange of British power in the world, which, as we have seen, does not threaten America, for German power, which certainly would.

Q. *If we are fighting against dictatorship and totalitarianism, what of Russia, which has always been a dictatorship whether under a Czar or a Stalin? What of China where dictators or war lords and not parliaments are the real rulers? Is not Russia's dictatorship as bad as Germany's?*

A. It may be worse or may have been worse in the past. But the question is not which is the more evil but which is the more dangerous. There have often been evil and oppressive dictatorships—the dictatorships of the Turkish Sultans, of the Russian Czars, of South American military despots. These in some respects, perhaps, were just as evil and oppressive as Hitler's government. But they were far less efficient and less powerful, and never really threatened the world. Bolshevist Russia, when the violently revolutionary mood was uppermost, was too incompetent to do so. The events since September 1, 1939, in which the Nazis have imposed their rule upon some twenty states, containing a total population immensely greater than that of Germany, prove that today the world is faced by the danger of domination by an evil but exceedingly efficient minority, the Nazi party. It is not Russia that has overcome twenty states; it is Germany. That phenomenon is due to a combination of circumstances: the genius for organization and slavish discipline possessed by the German people, the coming of new methods and instruments of warfare as the result of new inventions like the airplane which the Germans were the first to seize and apply thoroughly, and above all to the fact that the non-German world, already weak in its resistance because divided by its old nationalisms and animosities, was still further weakened in its resistance by its divisions over the Nazi philosophy itself. In every country that Hitler has conquered there were some who favored his creed, favored it because it seemed preferable to Communism. The hesitations which arose because people could not make up their minds which evil they detested most were among the things which gave him power.

Let us grant, for the sake of argument, that Russian Communism is an evil thing. So be it. What are we of the United Nations to do about it? Shall we let Hitler conquer Russia so completely that the Nazi empire is brought to within fifty miles of American territory; and let him set up his "Vichy" governments in Russia, with all its resources at his command? It would be the end of us.

As to China she has been going through the growing pains of an ancient Empire, much of it having remained in a medieval sleep, in conditions like those of Europe in the Middle Ages, changing into a modern republic. The spirit of the Chinese people is essentially democratic; they have still to work out the form of democratic institution which suits them best. If they are conquered by Japan a quarter of the world's population becomes the instrument of Asiatic totalitarianism; an instrument for the subjugation of America, among other democracies.

Men differ about the meaning of democracy. In this country men dispute as to whether it is or should be a "democracy" or a "republic." China may not be a democracy in our sense, but every observer of Chinese life is agreed that the Chinese secure for themselves the essentials of a free and democratic life; this is true of much of the village life of India, while Russia has set before herself the ideal of a life which shall give not merely political but economic freedom. All these efforts may be more or less successful, but they are all fighting for the freedom to go on making the effort; but if that struggle should fail they would not even have the right to make the effort, and they could be used as tools for the destruction of our freedom. There may possibly be dangers for us in their combination as a single group threatening the West; there would certainly be dangers for us if they became the instruments of a Japanese or German overlordship or an overlordship shared by those two powers in a sort of totalitarian condominium. If free, those peoples are likely to make their way toward democracy: they have shown already that

LET THE PEOPLE KNOW

the "unchanging East" is a myth. If conquered by the totalitarians we know that they become tools for our destruction.

Q. *If Russia, of nearly two hundred million people, and China, of four hundred million, are victorious and join with India of four hundred million, a good deal more than half the world's land and about half its population will form a bloc which has never in history known democratic institutions. Does the prospect look like making the world very safe for democracy?*

A. This of course is our old friend the Yellow Peril. All experience so far would prove it to be a bogey. Asiatics are not united among themselves against the West. On the contrary, one great Asiatic people, the Chinese, are allied with Americans and British and other Europeans, against another Asiatic people, the Japanese. In India, Moslem confronts Hindu with a deep gulf between them.

If it be true that there is a possibility of some great Eastern or Eurasian combination of these three powers, it becomes the more urgent that the West prove itself capable of unity. If Western civilization—American, both Latin and Anglo-Saxon, French, British, Scandinavian, Italian, Spanish, Dutch, Czech, Southern Slav, and in the Commonwealths of the Pacific, the Philippines, Australia, New Zealand—if these can act as a unit in defense, they would always, in terms of power, be able to counterbalance any such combination as that indicated in the question, if any "counterbalance" should be called for. Of course, the Asiatic peoples may prove to be as foolish as those of the West have been, and misuse their power. But that danger will be reduced to a minimum by proof that we of the West can co-operate for the maintenance of that right to life which we offer to Asia, as well as claim for ourselves.

Q. *If Russia beats Germany, will not Russia dominate and direct any future German revolution, giving it a Communist turn? And if the New China and the New India turn toward Communism, as some of the Chinese and Indian leaders threaten, will not Communism then dominate the world?*

A. The question whether or no Russia would continue "world

revolution" was fought out between Stalin and Trotsky—with the results we know. Russia may not have given up the slogans of the world-wide revolution but she has long since given it up as a foreign policy. All reliable witnesses now concur in the statement that of recent years Russian nationalism—the pride in Russia as a nation, the desire to build it up as a powerful and independent state—has enormously increased, and the interest in foreign economic revolution correspondingly diminished. As recently as July, 1942, Maurice Hindus writing to the New York *Times* has emphasized this fact again and again in his dispatches. The ideology is no longer mainly Bolshevist or Marxist; it is Russian. Novelists, poets, writers that in the early days of the Bolshevist order were utterly taboo as "bourgeois" are now once more being read with avidity. It is clear that the Moscow government is either building up or allowing to grow up a popular mood in tune with the changed foreign policy.

Russia has just concluded a twenty-year Treaty with Britain; in which, during that long period, the nature of Anglo-Russian co-operation, political and economic, is forecast. Does anyone suppose that Britain would lend herself to the Bolshevization of Europe? Or that she would have entered into this close and prolonged arrangement if such association would aid in "world revolution"?

After this war Russia will be in a state of devastation and economic need difficult for a Westerner to imagine. Much of the work of twenty years will have been destroyed. She will be compelled in a sense to make a fresh start. She will make it, having been saved from German defeat, in part by the aid of the United States and Britain. The old Bolshevist allegations that the capitalist world is leagued against her to destroy her will have been completely discredited by the events of the war itself. This new start will therefore be made in a mood from which a great deal of the old mutual suspicions and hostilities will have been swept away. Given the fact that in this temper Russia will need above all the material help of the United States and Britain in the task of reconstruction, is it likely that Stalin who for long has been an enemy of the "world revolution" idea,

would encourage forms of revolution in Germany which would alien-
ate the nations—America and Britain—whom he will most need
economically, and, probably also, politically.[1]

From the moment that Russia becomes more closely associated
for purposes of defense with "capitalist" states, much of what we
have disapproved in Russia will disappear. Plainly Russia will not
want to destroy or weaken those upon whom it depends for its own
defense; it will pass the word along to the Communists in Britain
and the United States to cease subversive activities and to aid in the
defensive activities. (Communists are already taking this line.) The
theory that "capitalists" must in all circumstances be enemies will
be abandoned—is already being abandoned.

As a vassal of Germany, organized and directed by Germany, Russia can be infinitely perilous. As a state dependent for its defense
against Germany upon the aid of Western bourgeois nations, like
Britain and America, it ceases to be a danger to Western civilization.
As to being non-Christian, most of the world is non-Christian, is
either Buddhist or Confucian or Mohammedan or Jewish. Conquest
of Russia by the state which has inaugurated the new paganism of
Rosenberg and his colleagues, who describe Jesus as a Jewish tramp,
will not make it more Christian.

Q. *If there are risks for American democracy in staying at home, are
there not greater risks still in being drawn into every foreign complication?*

A. This country *has* been drawn into "foreign complications" in
most tragic and disastrous fashion precisely *because* it was not committed. If it had been committed, if Japan and Germany had known
from the first that the United States would, in company with Britain
and a score of other nations, instantly oppose any aggression, then
the aggression would not have been attempted, or, if attempted,
could not have got very far. Once more, if the nations—including
America—had been ready to "do early what later they were com-

---

[1] There is a story, perhaps apocryphal, of Stalin and Cripps. Stalin was
asked how he had got along with Cripps. "Splendidly, splendidly," replied
Stalin; and then added: "But tell me, why, in Heaven's name does Cripps go
around talking all this Communism?"

pelled to do, they would not have been compelled to do it." The "complications" would have been kept within more manageable proportions, and we should probably not have been involved as we are.

As to mixing in foreign wars, for considerably over a century America has repeatedly pledged itself to fight in foreign wars. For, again and again, with the approval of the American people, the Monroe Doctrine has been proclaimed as an essential part of this country's foreign policy. America promised to intervene if the security of any one of twenty nations on this hemisphere is threatened from Europe. President Cleveland even risked conflict with Britain in order to champion Venezuela in a frontier dispute of no very great importance.

The Monroe Doctrine has prevented foreign nations from picking off the weaker American Republics one by one (as Hitler has done with the Continental nations of Europe) and thus obtaining footholds upon this continent whence some great European power could attack this country.

But please note that this policy of Monroe which, in the American view, has so greatly contributed to the security of this country, has been maintained for considerably over a hundred years without war. Just because foreign nations really believe that the United States meant business (and had the British Fleet behind it), the policy was not challenged and it was never necessary to put into execution the threat to go to war.

If Great Britain had said in 1934 to Mussolini: "We shall, being signatories to the Covenant, defend Ethiopia exactly as though it were Kenya or Kent," there would have been no Ethiopian war; for, if Mussolini had really believed that the country would be defended by Britain as Kent would be defended, he would not have attacked it.

For nearly a century and a quarter Americans have stood by the principle that the defense of certain other nations—those of Latin America—is an indispensable part of the defense of the United States. That measure of collective security by which this country has said: "We shall regard an attack on any American nation as an attack upon us"—has proved workable and effective, *without war*.

But note this distinction: while this country would go to war to prevent a German occupation of Argentina, it could afford, the isolationists told us, to remain indifferent if the Germans occupy Ireland.

Why that particular distinction? Irish ports are very much nearer to the United States (a fact which some Americans do not seem to know) than is Buenos Aires. The capture of the Argentine Navy by the Germans, or of Argentinian shipyards and airplane factories, would not greatly upset the balance of naval or air power in the world; but the capture of the British Navy and shipyards by the Germans, to be followed, of course, by the domination of Africa and India, would so shift power in the world as to place this country in mortal jeopardy. It is on the face of it a clear absurdity to say that it is a life-and-death matter for this country to defend Argentina or Chile from German occupation, that that is something for which American boys should be glad to die; but that it will not endanger this country for the Germans to take possession of Ireland, the Irish and British harbors and British shipyards and factories and all the harbors and resources of Africa, and to push across Russia to the Pacific coast, establishing bases within a couple of score miles of the American coast. If there were good reasons behind the Monroe Doctrine, if, in certain circumstances it is necessary for America's defense for her to pledge herself to the defense of nations some of which are by sea at least six thousand miles away, it may well be wise for her security to pledge American power to the defense of certain nations that happen to be very much nearer the United States.

The fact that the world has become smaller, that space is being annihilated, that circumstances alter, compels corresponding alterations in policies like that embodied in the Monroe Doctrine. The purpose of that doctrine was to defend this hemisphere against the totalitarian powers of Monroe's day, the members of the Holy Alliance. America was able to do this thanks to the fact that it was to Britain's interest to lend the support of her Navy to the enforcement of that policy. As Adams, Jefferson, Madison, and Monroe all agreed at the time, that policy would have been impossible without the support of the British Navy. In their day, just after its defeat of Napoleon, that Navy was supreme, unchallenged. Today the fall of Britain might put much of its Navy—and certainly its ports and shipbuilding yards—as well as those of France and Holland, Belgium, Norway, Italy, and Russia, in German hands. On the face of it that event would threaten the United States more today than, say, the German seizure of Brazil. Are Americans in the future to be pledged to go to war for the latter, but to give notice to Germany that, so far as any action by this country is concerned, she will not be interfered with in her steady destruction of British shipping, the final taking over of the British Isles, the absorption of Africa, India, Russia, Asia? Such a series of conquests would be a strategic threat to the United States far more serious than the European occupation of several South American states.

Q. *If we are drawn into these never-ending conflicts, will not the very complexity of the issues make it necessary to withdraw decisions from Congress? Does not power to decide foreign policy inevitably mean power to decide all policies—domestic and foreign alike— since foreign matters involve war, and once at war, all domestic matters must yield to its needs? Is this the way to make democracy secure?*

A. First we—the United Nations—will not be drawn into war at all if we unite in the obvious intention to oppose the war maker. He will not challenge a combination of that power. Both world wars have arisen because the aggressors were able to take their victims one by one; because those victims did not make it plain beforehand that they would stand together on the principle that an attack on one would be regarded as an attack on all.

The idea that commitments mean increasing the danger of war is a complete fallacy. The nations which were drawn into war twice within a quarter of a century were nations that had avoided commitments like a plague—nations which had for years insisted on keeping their hands free, on the avoidance of all entanglements. The one thing which would almost certainly have prevented war would have been a firm commitment to fight the nation that refused peaceful settlement of a dispute and embarked upon aggression.

Hitler's dictatorship extended to the United States. It was he who forced this country (before war) to introduce conscription, tax itself as it has never been taxed before, to turn its economic and social system upside down—all this was forced upon the American people by the edicts issued by a dozen men in Berlin over whom this country has no sort of control. Even though Germany had made no war upon this country, the long arm of Hitler had reached into every American purse, the interior of every American home. These are very domestic matters indeed: but decisions of American domestic policy were imposed by Hitler while still at peace with America. Is this "independence"?

To say that because war destroys democracy we will not go to war means, of course, that we will not defend our country at all. For "defense means war," if the country is attacked. Would you refuse to bring about a state of war if the country were attacked because "war would be the end of democracy"? But in fact war does not mean, with free people, the end of democracy. All witnesses agree that both America and Britain, in the midst of war, have preserved the essentials of democracy. There is freedom of speech, freedom to level criticisms—sometimes very bitter—at the government; freedom to listen to German propaganda over the radio; to debate; to bring grievances to Congress or to Parliament. Perhaps the best answer to the suggestion implied in the question is to compare the state of France today with that of Britain. France surrendered rather than go on with war, and obtained "peace." That peace has meant the end of every semblance of democracy, of parliamentary government, of popular right; a Fascist order which has swept away the gains of the Revolution. It has meant a government to which 90 per cent of the people are bitterly opposed, so bitterly that every day Frenchmen give their lives to oppose it. Compare this with the devotion and unity of the American people behind their president; the Chinese people in the fifth year of the war; the British people in their support of Churchill; in these examples we have daily demonstration of how willingly and democratically free peoples can defend their institutions.

Q. *We know something at least of our own problems—the trusts, labor, farming issues, social security—but how can the American voter and the American Congress pass upon the rights and wrongs of struggles in Europe, Asia, and Africa?*

A. The American voter and Congress do not have to pass upon such issues. All they have to decide is that the issues shall not be settled by war of the stronger upon the weaker. In 1931, China was ready to submit the differences with Japan to arbitration; just as in 1934, Ethiopia was ready to submit any grievances that Italy might have to arbitration. It was not the business of the powers to decide who was right and who was wrong in the dispute but to decide that neither should settle it by war upon the other; to say: "Since China —or Ethiopia, as the case may be—is ready to seek peaceful settlement, third-party judgment, court, arbitration, and is nevertheless being subject to threat of war, we shall defend those states, until the aggressor does accept peaceful settlement." It is not this sort of "intervention" which "involves" a country like the United States to the largest extent; it is complete neutrality which has had the result of involving the country, has turned its whole economy upside down, compelled it to alter, completely and radically, its way of life. The other policy, if carried through, would probably have maintained peace and prevented the outbreak of the present war, and would consequently have kept this country much clearer of entanglements in the disputes of Europe than neutrality in fact has done. Absence of obligation does not mean absence of liability.

Q. *If we unite with Britain do we not unite with the British Empire also, and take responsibility for India, Palestine, Africa; go, in fact, into the Empire business?*

A. As shown in one of the chapters of this book Britain is going out of the Empire business, turning territories like Canada and Australia into independent states; with India to follow so soon as internal difficulties in India are not likely to involve the United

Nations in the kind of difficulty presented by an independent Eire that withholds the use of harbors necessary for effective defense and adopts a neutrality which endangers its neighbors. America is already, as part of her clear defensive interest, helping to defend Australia and India (to say nothing of Britain itself). To face the fact that anarchy and chaos will in any case present America intermittently with the kind of problem now confronting her is to face the conclusion that the best thing to do about it is to help end the chaos and the anarchy.

America does not want to mix up in the internal affairs of India, but she does want to be able, with the other guardians of world peace, to prevent great territories falling into the hands of aggressors, potential or actual. It would suffice perhaps for this purpose to command the Indian Ocean and that would be done with suitable airfields and naval bases in Malaya, Burma, Ceylon, India. Those bases might be held, not by the United States, not by Britain, but by the United Nations, represented perhaps by a Defense Board sitting in Washington or Singapore. Would it be beneath India's dignity to cede or lease such naval and air bases to an international body? It was not beneath Britain's dignity to lease important bases on British territory to the United States. Why should not India be prepared to do for the United Nations—a great international body in which India herself had membership—what Britain has been ready to do for a foreign power, a foreign power moreover with whom she has in the past been at war and by whom she has been beaten? (It is supposed to be more difficult for the vanquished than for the victor to forget old quarrels.)

Perhaps in the earlier stages of the world reorganization (a reorganization whose beginnings are taking place during the war) a Defense Committee whose membership should include Americans as well as Indian and British could direct the transition of Indian policy. Obviously the American members of such a committee would occupy a powerful position which would go some way to meet misgivings in America as to whether Britain's Indian policy is all that it ought to be.

Q. *If we federate with Britain and its Empire, what of the king, and hereditary peers, titles, class divisions, and distinctions—things which don't go at all well with the American tradition of republican and democratic equality we have maintained ever since we kicked the British king and the British aristocrats out of this country?*

A. Suppose instead of "federation" we talked, first of all, about an understanding for mutual aid against aggression and a continuation, until things settle down, of the wartime boards and commissions. They will have to go on in any case for a very long time. Many difficulties have arisen in the operation of these international boards— Canadian-American, Australian-American, Indian-American, British-American. But it is safe to say that on not one single occasion has a difficulty ever arisen because of the fact that Britain is a monarchy, or, as it was once described more correctly, "a crowned republic." Britain has proved that in the things which matter she can be extremely radical and democratic. Her parliamentary system, in which the government, including the prime minister, have to give an account of their stewardship constantly to her people's representatives, and can be turned out by them from one day to another, has features which are more ruthlessly democratic than the operation sometimes of the United States constitution. The king is a symbol and a survival, but a politically convenient survival. He is a sort of national chairman whose function it is to say, "By the rules of the meeting, it is your turn to speak, Mr. Jones," or, "Your turn to form a government, Mr. Baldwin"; and a chairman who is designated by lot—the lottery of birth. It works; and that is the supreme consideration with the British who care little for logical neatness or symmetry in their constitutional arrangements. It is particularly convenient for a group of nations scattered over the earth, and so situated that elections for a common ceremonial head would hardly be practicable. The monarchy is a symbol, and symbols are important; as organized religion has learned. Even outside religion and politics we adopt symbols from the past, which, though they have lost in practice their original meaning are convenient. When we call a man "Mister" we are using a word which in its origin means "My

Master." We use the term, but we don't mean by it what it meant originally. Intercourse would probably be less easy, less courteous, less urbane, and the wheels of life be more subject to friction, if we did not adopt such means of lubrication. The British seem to have found that the retention of the old feudal forms tends to lubricate certain parts of the political and social machinery subject to friction. Retention of such forms engenders an atmosphere of respect and courtesy; much as the ceremonial of a court of law and the gown of the judge help maintain an atmosphere which makes for order and seriousness.

When America was fighting for her independence she welcomed help from the French monarchy (one of the most reactionary of history) and particularly from a French aristocrat, the Marquis de Lafayette. To mark her gratitude for aid given, America resorted to the hereditary principle: descendants of Lafayette are American citizens by right of birth, although they may be French citizens, born in France.

As to British titles, more and more are they becoming mere marks of distinction, medals which are pinned onto a man's name instead of to his coat. The whole principle of medals may be wrong, but every nation, including Soviet and Communist Russia, resorts to them.

Q. *Shall we have to share that brand of British Socialism which has grown up this last thirty years, with its dole, its vast unemployment insurance, its Labour Party, its grueling income tax—all to be added, perhaps, to our own New Deal? Do Americans really want that way of life?*

A. Since the British number forty-five millions and the Americans a hundred and thirty, since the British are poor and the Americans rich, with all the advantages of natural resources and great area on the American side, why should it be assumed that the preponderance of influence in any combination must be British and not American? America will be the senior partner in any Anglo-American partnership. It indicates a very serious inferiority complex to assume that the British are bound to lead and the Americans to follow. Why should not America do a little leading?

Even the British Dominions like Canada and Australia, New Zealand and South Africa have all developed their distinctive forms of national life, which differ from the British. In any closer association between the British Commonwealth and the American Union, the Americanization of the British nations rather than the Anglicizing of America, is likely to be the result.

Q. *Does equality of economic opportunity mean that Asiatics are to be admitted freely to the United States and that goods made under the American standard of wages have to compete with goods made by coolie labor?*

A. Neither Asiatics nor Europeans are admitted freely to the United States. The days of completely free migration for any people are over. What Asiatics in fact demand is that discrimination shall not be on a basis merely of race, with an insulting implication that they are inferior. It should be quite possible to work out a quota system which does not involve race discrimination and would not endanger the American standard of life. For generations the high wages of the North in America have had to compete with low rates of Negroes in the South, and, on the whole have managed to do so successfully. Low wages, whether in India or Alabama, do not mean low production costs, and Americans have shown that they can compete with "pauper labor." Moreover, the I.L.O. of the League of Nations has in the past done a great deal to equalize conditions of labor throughout the world. It could, if supported, do more.

More and more will exports and imports come under government control and regulation, not through tariffs, but through methods of licenses and bulk purchase. Immediately foreign trade is thought of in terms of commodities which both parties want, the less terrifying do differing wage rates appear. If Brazil is offering coffee in exchange for certain manufactured goods, it is certain that the American negotiators of the deal will not say to the Brazilians, "Please give us as little coffee as possible in return for the goods we offer." The

American negotiators instead of trying to keep out goods, which is the purpose of tariffs, will want to get in as much as possible; that is to say, will try to get them cheaply. The extension of such a system of "managed" foreign trade will change attitudes both toward tariffs and the cheapness of foreign products.

Q. Are we to re-create the League we refused to have anything to do with twenty years ago, or make a Union Now with Britain, or with other democracies, or with all the members of the United Nations, or what?

A. The implied assumption behind that question (and others like it) is that at the end of the war we shall find conditions broadly resembling those which marked the end of the last war: the belligerents, Allied and Axis alike, in a position to be represented by relatively stable governments with complete authority within their boundaries, able to sign treaties of peace, and then enter into the kind of discussion which went on for years following the last armistice, when fifty nations could gather together and debate elaborately the articles of a League of Nations.

The conditions which we may expect to follow upon the collapse of the Axis powers in this war will bear hardly any resemblance to such a picture, and we would do well to get it out of our minds, if we are to be ready to take the kind of steps which almost certainly will be necessary.

Consider for a moment what the occupied countries will have gone through, taking Poland, Yugoslavia, and Czechoslovakia as examples. Their frontiers have been torn and juggled with, not merely by the Axis powers but in certain cases by national minorities within the frontiers; vast transfers of population have taken place; thousands taken from a given area and other thousands brought into it. At the end of the war the peoples will have been living for years under a terror difficult for Americans to conceive; men, women, and children by the hundred thousand subjected to obscene tortures in the attempt to extract information involving the betrayal of friends or relatives to the Gestapo; mass killings in which whole communities have been wiped out, as Indian sav-

ages in the seventeenth century wiped out New England town-
ships. Hundreds of thousands have been torn from their homes
and transported into actual chattel slavery in some distant country—a systematized extermination of peoples carried out with the
cold and ruthless determination to bring about the actual physical
destruction of nations. Girls have been seized and bred to the
Herrenvolk, as cows might be bred to prize bulls. In addition to
all that, with the breakdown of transportation and communication
which will mark the point of Axis collapse, will come an intensifi-
cation of famine and pestilence.

At that moment of Nazi collapse continental Europe is likely
to be a blazing inferno, a hell of hate and vengeance. Local leaders, developed in the years of underground resistance, will in many
cases attempt to take charge and repudiate the authority of the
governments now in exile in London. (In the case of France the
creation of an acceptable provisional government to succeed the
Vichy gang will be especially difficult.) Revolutionary governments—some of them inspired by little local Hitlers—may be
mushrooming up all over Europe, using the chaos to install themselves in power so as to present the Allies with a *fait accompli.*

Now, it is pretty obvious that unless these volcanic upheavals
are controlled at the beginning, they may get utterly out of hand,
and we may face a black chaos in which the peace may be lost,
not in the way it was lost before, but just as disastrously so far as
future freedom and order are concerned. More than usually will
freedom at that time depend on order.

To prevent this kind of disorganization, there must be some center of authority able to take instant decisions, to act rapidly, to impose itself in the solution of local conflicts; to fly a military force
to an area of disorder; to stop indiscriminate massacre or lynching
of Germans (for, paradoxically, to defend Germans may be one of
the indispensable conditions for laying the foundations of a good
peace); to supply food to a famine area, doctors, and medical sup-
plies to one stricken with pestilence.

If in this early part of the post-war period we are afraid of authority, afraid of giving power to such organs of control as we have, or try to withhold power for fear it might be misused—if we make that kind of error at the beginning, we may find later that we cannot make either a League, or a Federation, or any other form of international government; find that we cannot make peace.

At that early stage of peace making the United States might once more usefully recall the type of action by which, from time to time, this country has helped to save democracy and national freedom on this hemisphere—the type of action illustrated in the history of the Monroe Doctrine, for instance. When the United States extended her protection over all American republics she did so without consulting them, well aware that many of them were not democracies at all. She did this in private agreement with Great Britain. If all the forms of democratic action had had to be followed—consultation and agreement with every American republic concerned, formal treaty with Great Britain, to be ratified formally by the Senate—if that had been the method of initiating the Monroe Doctrine, it would probably never have come into being. Democracy can sometimes only be saved by action which in form is undemocratic.

The organs of authority necessary for securing order after the collapse of the Axis will have been brought into being by the needs of war; will exist in the unified command which (let us hope) by that time will have been achieved; in the various inter-allied bodies of supply and economic control set up for the purposes of the war. These bodies must not be dissolved almost immediately the cease fire sounds (as they were after the last war). They must be retained and adapted to the purposes of this preliminary period, which will be one not so much of reconstruction as of rescue—rescue from famine, pestilence, violence.

The first great need will be food, clothing, fuel, with shipping and transport to get those things to the areas where they will be most needed. They will be mainly in the hands of the United States, Canada, Britain, Australia, New Zealand, South Africa.

Those countries will also be, towards the close of the war, the main producers of munitions.

The first condition of sound foundations for peace is that those countries at least shall remain sufficiently united to act as a unit in carrying out the preliminary task of rescue.

Such unity and agreement ought not to be difficult. It is sometimes much easier to secure agreement on acts than on policies or theories—as President Roosevelt has shown in his conduct of foreign policy again and again. If in the sending of troops to Iceland, or in the Destroyer-Bases deal, he had had to secure the preliminary assent of Congress the debate might have gone on interminably. But, the step having been taken, the public quickly gave its approval, because a principle or policy which is illustrated by an act is much easier to grasp than one not so illustrated.

If therefore the organs of the United Nations which have been or will have been created for the purposes of war continue to function after the war, and act in the way described for the preliminary period of peace, they may grow into international institutions later destined to become a rudimentary world government. Whether that government should take the form broadly of the League as we have known it, or should be more of a Federation; or should be rather a group of nations bound together for mutual security along the lines of the Locarno group of treaties, will depend upon the degree of success achieved in meeting these first postwar conditions. If the United Nations fail in that preliminary task, it is unlikely that they would be able to come together again for the working of a larger, more elaborate, more difficult international organization.

One early criticism of the development above outlined is bound to be that because the United States, Canada, Australia, New Zealand, South Africa, and Britain will at the close of the war be the main repositories of food stuffs, and such raw materials as wool and cotton for clothing, and the main holders of shipping and munitions, they will therefore dominate the scene and create misgivings in the minds of Latin America, Russia, and China. What is the remedy? For those English-speaking countries *not* to agree? *Not* to achieve, in a world where agreement seems so immeasurably difficult, a beginning of agreement by making it first of all where the forces of history or tradition or language have made it easiest?

The course of wisdom is to use agreement between the nations just enumerated as a stepping stone to wider agreement. Already in most of the Inter-Allied bodies engaged in the war tasks representation is given to South America, Russia, China, India, and others of the United Nations. Of course they should be associated as closely as possible in the task of rescue and reconstruction above described. By carrying out that task together, habits of international co-operation will be developed. If economic assistance to Russia and China is on a generous scale, confidence between those countries and the West is likely to be strengthened. (Canada, so long hesitant in her relations with Russia, is already sending great quantities of wheat to the latter country.)

Certain other features of policy are indicated. The enemy individuals actually responsible for the terror above described should be treated as criminals: seized, held for trial, tried, and on condemnation punished, mainly with the capital penalty. But the German people as a whole should be extended the same relief from famine and pestilence, and the same defense from lawless violence, as others. The more generous we are in the treatment of the German people economically, the more likely is political severity— the occupation of Germany during a longish period, for instance— to be effective. We should not commit the German faults. No children should be punished, or made to suffer, if it can be avoided. Babies are neutral. This should not prevent on occasion the employment of the economic sanction which the organs of the United Nations would hold in their hands. To obtain relief a local government would have to conform to the conditions laid down by the United Nations.

Let us by all means discuss the kind of international government likely to work best, and be acceptable to the peoples; more especially let us clarify the principles which must animate any international constitution, if it is to preserve peace and permit freedom. But let us also remember that we shall never reach that future international government, however good the blueprint of it which we may now draw up, unless the day to day steps of policy in the early postwar period are marked by greater wisdom than was our behavior in the period immediately following the last armistice. Whether or not this time the direction of day to day policy avoids the errors which were committed on the last occasion, whether or not we destroy our Wilsons once more, and once more, blaming our failures on each other, or on some convenient scapegoats, turn to isolationism and Neutrality Acts, will depend upon the degree of John Citizen's understanding of the principles these pages have attempted to unfold.